CAREER BUILDING:

How to STAND OUT,
Get Ahead & Get Noticed!

By **Marja Lee Freeman**
The Employment Lady

D1399702

Disclaimer: This book is designed to provide information as it relates to employment and career development. The publisher and the author are not offering legal advice. The strategies contained herein may not be suitable for your situation. You should consult with a human resource professional where appropriate. While the author and the publisher have used every effort in preparing this book, they make no representations or warranties with respect to the outcome of any situation and cannot be held liable or responsible for any damages allegedly caused, directly or indirectly by the information in this book.

Before making decisions concerning your legal rights or actions in the workplace, first consult with the Equal Employment Opportunity Commission as it relates to employment issues.

© 2014 Marja Lee Freeman Consulting, LLC
All Rights Reserved

ISBN: 1466337966
ISBN 13: 9781466337961
Library of Congress Control Number: 2011916685
CreateSpace Independent Publishing Platform
North Charleston, South Carolina

ACKNOWLEDGMENTS

Wow, I've finally made it! This has been the most important project of my life. I know it sounds clichéd, but it's true. You can't do anything of this magnitude without the love, support, and prayers of the people who surround you.

To my parents, John and Pearl G. Lee, who gave me life and the courage to believe that I could do anything because of their love, commitment and support.

To Cynthia Evans, who helped me with the first draft of this book when I had the initial idea, which comprised only twenty-two pages at the time. We were also just beginning our journey with the Laurie Mitchell Empowerment and Career Center. It seems the three of us – me, you and LMECC have blossomed into our full potential.

To my second parents, Apostle Leroy V. Washington Sr. and Evangelist Lila Washington, who prayed that the Lord would use my talents to His glory.

And finally, to my husband, Donald Freeman—you predicted my book would be successful, and I believed it would came to pass. Without your love, encouragement, and cookin' (this man throws down in the kitchen), I would not have had enough strength to make this happen.

ABOUT THIS BOOK

Everyone has to work, right? At least that's what your parents have probably told you. Many of us in the workforce have never been trained to work; someone just told us to get a job. It's a common belief that once you get a job, you're Okay. However, that's not always the case. Still, we're just ecstatic that we've been chosen. Getting a job and keeping it, however, are two different things. Statistically, more people are fired for people-related issues than work-related issues.

The primary focus of this book is to give people—high school college students, self-employed or underemployed workers, temporary or transitioning employees—insight concerning employment mistakes that are never brought to your attention.

Working with people is a requirement if you want to be successfully employed. Building your career begins with building rapport. People need to be comfortable with you. If they are comfortable with you, they will enjoy working with you, and that's important. There are many small nuances to working with people that we are never taught in school. But these nuances are the building blocks of relationships and are critical to the success of your career.

This book will give you the tools to learn how to **STAND OUT, GET AHEAD,** and **GET NOTICED** no matter where you begin your career. Your degree gives you knowledge, but experience + knowledge build…

Professional Power!

ABOUT THE AUTHOR

I must admit, I didn't start out in the job of my dreams. I began working as a car washer at the early age of twelve. I asked my Granddaddy Green for a loan so I could buy some ice cream from the ice cream truck. The first question he asked me was "Are you wurkin'?" He spoke with an old Southern accent. I looked at him quizzically and said, "Well...no."

He said, "Then how are you gonna' pay Granddaddy back if I loan you the money?"

That's when it came to me to offer to wash his car. Back then, cars were as large as city blocks, and Granddaddy drove an old 1960 Cadillac. I figured that my offer should hold me for four ice creams—he agreed!

That, ladies and gentlemen, was the beginning of my quest for a job. I didn't realize it, but I was then forging my destiny as a sole proprietor. I had a number of self-run businesses in my youth. I washed cars, cut grass, babysat, was a drugstore runner, cleaned houses for the elderly, and worked as a live-in nanny, school bus driver, court stenographer, typist, and receptionist. While serving in the US Army, I was an administrative assistant to the headquarters commander. After returning to civilian life, I became a staff instructor, résumé writer, job placement specialist and trainer, employment director, and ultimately, a professional speaker/trainer and career coach. That's seventeen jobs, man!

I actually began my speaking career in 1990, when I saw a segment on the local news about a homeless shelter known as the Mitch Synder Shelter in Washington, DC. The segment reported that the residents were starting their lives all over again, and many of them didn't have jobs. What began as a ministry became the foundation of my career consulting business. I began to produce and conduct workshops such as "The Art of Finding and Keeping a Job." The workshops were a success!

After receiving many inspirational letters, hugs, kisses, candy, and tears of joy, I expanded my services to include designing courses, seminar conferences with local and national professional seminars and conferences.

Helping people to achieve their dreams gave me a special feeling, and I realized that helping others achieve their dreams was my destiny. I stretched out and began to build my business as a motivational speaker and trainer. I hope this book motivates, inspires, and challenges you to move forward in your path to career success in your own life.

Marja Lee Freeman
The Employment Lady

TABLE OF CONTENTS

♦ Give Yourself Permission to Turn the Day Off

♦ Don't give Anyone the Power to Ruin Your Day

WHAT AUDIENCES ARE SAYING:

Zully Goya, US Comptroller of the Currency

Hi Marja! I wanted to just say thank you for helping me with my résumé; once I applied your recommendations, I immediately got several phone calls for interviews. Wow, what a difference!

Darlene Nelson, Junior Project Manager

I wanted to let you know that after attending your workshop, I went back to work and implemented several of your recommendations. I am pleased to announce that I was just promoted to Junior Project Manager and I have only been here for six months! Your insight and wisdom are second-to-none.

Dennis James, Business Management, University College

"I had no idea the difference a résumé could make in just getting a callback. The résumé samples were great!"

Rhonda Fleming, College of Education, University College

"Marja Lee Freeman is a born communicator. Her presentations are real life situations/experiences. Her passion in her radiates and transforms the participants to go forward and be better people in their perspective environments. She's Awesome!"

Denese D. Straughn, Administrative Assistant, Faculty and Employee Assistance Program

Marja's career counseling expertise, combined with her instructional style make her a powerful teacher on the daily challenges within the work place. She has much to offer for those entering the job market - many for the first time!"

Amanda McElwee, Geisinger Health System

Words cannot describe how amazing Marja is as a leader! Every word that came out of her mouth is something I will take with me and use in my everyday career!"

Margaret McMullen, Professional Trainer, Leader Development Institute

"Bright, funny, and extremely knowledgeable, Marja Lee Freeman captures the attention of any audience. Her reputation precedes her. If you are looking for a professional trainer who will "knock your socks off," Marja Lee is the one you want. Her positive, uplifting message will touch every member of the audience. You go, Marja Lee!"

Wanda McCallum, Professional Trainer

"Marja Lee Freeman charismatically connects with the participants. Imagine the comic wit of Eddie Murphy combined with Oprah Winfrey's ability to connect and engage people. If you really want to wow your group, bring in Marja Lee Freeman. She will have your group laughing, learning, and feeling inspired to make changes in their lives."

Sara Skorak, Union Hospital, Cecil County

Marja's experience and techniques are priceless! She keeps it high energy and on topic. I thoroughly enjoyed her workshops! She is positive and motivational. What a fabulous experience. Many thanks to Marja's guidance and skills.

CHAPTER 1

YOUR VISION FOR YOUR FUTURE

Building anything first begins with vision. Your vision is what you expect something to look like when it's completed. Building a career starts with the same concept—a blueprint on paper—the foundation to your destination. In this book, I will discuss the schematics of building a career in any field. It will begin with some basic tools—some of which you may already know and some of which you may not know.

Considering we live in a technological age, some of the techniques I am going to share have been recently developed such as uploading your résumé and completing your application online. Connecting with employers is as simple as hitting the send button. Your career blueprint will be unique in that it will incorporate your specifications, your talents, your experience, and your life's work in everything you've ever done. It cannot be replicated, copied, or changed to suit someone else's experience. As you go through these lessons, each chapter will offer you strategies to:

◆ help you navigate the job market from high school and beyond
◆ give you the tools and strategies to find and build a career that fits your personality
◆ supply you with the requirements for building a résumé that gets noticed
◆ equip you to understand employer expectations
◆ reveal marketing strategies that position you to get noticed and promoted
◆ help you manage your time effectively in the workplace

- build working relationships with your coworkers and clients
- get past negative stigma in the workplace
- effectively use techniques to handle everyday office dilemmas and even office politics
- determine what to do if you work with people you don't like and lastly
- websites that will help you get in the door the job you want

Everybody Has to Start Somewhere

Finding a job is the most difficult thing most of us will ever achieve, short of climbing Mt. Everest or running a marathon, that is. Growing up, we've all heard the "You need to get a job and do something with your life" speech. With that in mind, off we go to take what we can get.

But what would the perfect job look like for you? Would you want to travel around the world? Be a movie star or a musician? A chef at a five-star restaurant? A nurse at a retirement home? They all sound great. First, let's start with the premise: *There's no such thing as the perfect job.* It's really about finding the right position for you—a position that will allow you to use your gifts and talents.

What do You Want to Be?

You can probably remember when you were little and someone would ask you, "What do you want to be when you grow up?" We knew exactly what we wanted to do.

When a child says, "I wanna' be in the circus," that child may only see the huge elephants, the ringmaster, the magicians, and the clowns that performed at the show. But someone actually gets paid to clean up…um, elephant gifts, as well as the trash after the crowd is gone. As children, we don't understand that everyone doesn't get the high-profile, fun jobs. However, using the circus (or whatever your passion is) as a platform is a great beginning. Determining what about the circus pulls your interest could be the beginning of your career development. Is it the animals, the audience, the artistry, the attention, the travel, the skill, or the pay?

Example: If you love animals, there are a number of jobs that will allow you to work with them outside of the circus. Determining why this career is of interest will help you start your career journey.

Here's my point: In every position, there are job responsibilities people will have to deal with that are time-consuming, irritating, stressful, or things they just don't want to do. If you cook, then you've got to put your hands in some pretty nasty lookin' stuff in order to make a great meal. If you work as a mechanic, prepare yourself for the daily grease. You see my point? It's just part of the job.

Doing the job helps to give you the hands-on experience that no one can teach you in college. One of the first jobs I had in my youth was babysitting. There was no better opportunity to make money while living on a military base. While it wasn't the job of my dreams, it taught me a lot of pertinent skills that would follow me throughout my career.

Here is a position description for childcare supervision:

- Candidate is commissioned to supervise, manage, and care for someone's most precious life.
- Must be willing to serve as secondary guardian representative in the absence of the primary parent.
- Candidate should be consistently punctual and time conscious to ensure naps are supervised.
- Great listening skills required. Candidate must be able to handle yelling, screaming, and tantrums from the backroom and be able to work with the child willing to throw an object at you.
- Must be able to supervise clients between the ages of six months to six years of age.
- Able to interpret sometimes unintelligible speaking style.
- Must be trained in areas of safety, CPR, as well as first aid.
- Willing to discipline if necessary.

- Able to think on your feet and under pressure during unexpected situations.
- Able to prepare food (preferably sandwiches), cook, clean up, and ensure that instructions are fully carried out.
- Candidate must have a strong stomach and be able to clean, wipe, and dispose of unpleasant "gifts."
- The candidate must be physically fit for activities such as running, jumping and working on the floor.
- The ideal candidate must be able to lift up to twenty pounds on shoulders and hips.
- Should be able to take down messages and keep house clean.
- Must feed and dress the client(s) appropriately.
- At the end of every shift, the candidate will be required to give a full and detailed report.

Kinda sounds a little like your job, huh? I firmly believe every position I've ever held has led me to my career in employment training. The experience of calming down a disgruntled four-year-old prepared me to deal with disgruntled adults without resorting to violence.

Finding Your True Calling

Determining where you want to be in your life is not just finding a job, but finding a "calling." According to *Webster's New College Dictionary*, the word *calling* is defined as either "a strong inner urge or impulse" or "an occupation: vocation."

While the dictionary doesn't say this, I believe that your calling is an innate talent that is ultimately the core of who you are. For some, it's singing; for others, it's writing; and for others, it's caring for the elderly.

As I travel around the country teaching workshops on finding your passion, one of the most consistent comments I hear is "I don't know what that [a calling] is for me. I'm not good at anything." *Everybody* has something that pulls on his or her heart—whether it's working with women who have been abused, sponsoring community blood drives, or working with children who can't read. Your calling doesn't have to be on a stage, it simply needs to be something you would do even if you didn't get paid to do it.

One resource that may help in the process of figuring out your calling is a book called *Discovering Your Purpose,* written by Ivy Haley. It offers an opportunity to take an inventory of your values, principles, and career path. One of the chapters focuses on "Sketching a Blueprint of Your Life Plan."

For more detailed steps you can take to determine what your calling might be, check out chapter 7, of the book "So, What Color *Is* Your Parachute?" Here you will find a number of online quizzes and other resources you can use to find out where your passion lies.

Dream It and Believe It!

Okay, after you have an idea of what your calling is, there are a few practical questions you need to ask yourself as you evaluate potential jobs. (Feel free to write in the book!)

1. How much money do you need (each week) to pay your bills with or without a family?
2. Could you afford to buy a home or rent on your current salary?
3. In what types of industries have you worked?
4. Where are you in your education and/or job training?
5. Where could you actually afford to live without financial stress?
6. Do you have a savings account as well as adequate insurance?
7. Could you pay bills not related to housing, student loans, healthcare, etc. on this salary?
8. If required, do you have money for unplanned expenses: car repair, hospital bills, second mortgage, car accidents, children's clothing, and education?
9. Do you hope to retire from this job?

Now, you've probably never thought of some of these questions, but you will need to be prepared for them. You need to be aware of the things you're not really ready for—like the hot water heater going out! Those types of unexpected events always mean money—cha-ching. Now, I'm not a finance expert—you'll need to check out Suzie Orman for expert advice on something like that, but my point is that you need to evaluate your financial needs first.

If you have never read Stephen Covey's powerful book, *The 7 Habits of Highly Effective People,* I recommend that you get your hands on it—or download it to your Kindle. The first most prominent point and beginning of your career-discovery starts with the first habit— "Begin with the End in Mind"!

PART 1

Time To Start Building

CHAPTER 3

HOW TO DEVELOP A STRATEGY THAT WORKS

A strategy is a system with a basic process that allows you to achieve something. It can be a daily structure that you follow in order to complete a task. We need a system for everything we do—from buying a home to going through the airport. If we're going through the airport, we need to bring photo identification, show a printed ticket or an electronic one, go through the security check-in process, board the plane, and follow all the proper procedures during the take-off and landing. Likewise, constructing anything requires architectural schematics. People who have been out of the workforce are also required to follow a system in order to get a job.

Unfortunately, some of us are still using the system that we utilized when we found our previous job, which can yield pretty disappointing results. If it worked before, why wouldn't it work again? As the years have passed and technology has expanded our horizons, the process of finding a job has also changed.

First things first. Make sure you have…

- ◆ access to a laptop, iPad, and flash drive
- ◆ a previous résumé and application (online résumé)
- ◆ connections and letters of recommendation or achievement
- ◆ names of at least four references (personal/professional), with addresses and detailed contact information
- ◆ a list of six positions of interest (researched)

♦ online job websites with your areas of interest

♦ an online calendar—or iPad or your favorite technology

♦ a method to track results and follow up

♦ self-motivation and patience

Research and Your Target Market

Now that you've got what you need to conduct your job search let's get started. Getting started entails a lot more than simply deciding what you want to be when you grow up and writing a résumé. (Of course, résumés are still vitally important, so they are covered later on in the book.)

Research is absolutely critical in determining your target market for employment. More importantly, it will help you narrow your search and maximize your time more effectively. Research comes in many forms and is not limited to online searching. Talking to someone who does a particular job for a living and asking about specific pros and cons can offer you just as much, if not more, insight.

People love to help others. I suggest you conduct mini-interviews with people who work in the field you are interested in getting into. Mini-interviews make people feel important and valuable that their knowledge can help you. As an example, you might do research and go to someone's LinkedIn page, find out about them, their industry and contact them online. One young lady did just that. She contacted me through LinkedIn to interview me about getting into the speaking industry. This allows the individual to contact you at their convenience.

Here are some of the questions to ask when doing research on a particular job:

♦ How long have you worked here?

♦ Did you find the position online or through a job connection?

♦ What type of education, training, certification, or testing is required?

♦ Did you do anything similar to this before you got the job?

- How long did it take you to actually find the position, apply, and get a response?
- What courses are necessary to work in the field?
- What are the most difficult aspects of the job?
- Did the position require an internship or volunteer experience?
- What is the average salary for someone in this field?
- What is the best part of doing what you do?

If you ask the right questions, you usually get a lot more insight than you would from a basic job description. Sometimes you end up learning that the position is a lot harder than it looks—ask any Mom!

Prepare Yourself Daily

Here are four simple steps that are essential to any job-hunting strategy:

- Determine the four most important things you intend to achieve each day.
- Determine four types of jobs you would be happy to do.
- Learn all you can while you can—take advantage of the information that is available to you.
- Establish and build relationships for the future, but cultivate your relationships from the past.

CHAPTER 4

FINDING A JOB IS A JOB

Yes, we have all heard this, but it's true! Finding a job in today's economy is a full-time job and requires an action plan you can put into place until you get one – and sometimes even after you get one. There's a major emotional component that goes with the process as well. It requires the four Ds: dreams, drive, determination, and destiny.

The more critical your economic situation, the more effort, time, and tenacity you're going to need. If you are unemployed or underemployed, you should dedicate at least four to six hours a day researching job opportunities. What do you mean, that's too much time? That's what an action plan is suppose to be. What else do you have to do? How much money you have in your bank account may determine how much energy you put into seeking your next job. But consider the last time you were on the job hunt. It was probably some time ago, right?

Think of it this way: the number of people you're competing against has tripled! You're competing against high school students, college students, early bloomers, late bloomers, grandma's bloomers, and baby boomers. Come on; that's a lot of folks. And you have to be prepared to offer employers something they can't get from anyone else—Y-O-U!

Set a schedule for yourself, and stick to it. If you utilize a schedule, it not only gives you incentive to keep looking, but prepares you mentally when an opportunity presents itself. Once our bodies and minds have gotten used to the idea of sleeping in, staying up late, and spending time without any real purpose of mind, our attitudes will follow the same pattern.

Once anger, depression, and hopelessness set in, your efforts begin to go downhill. A common mistake people make during the job search process is to send out résumés and fill out applications, but rarely keep track of their efforts. On the average, it takes between six to eight months to receive a response to an application, which is why a savings account is critical. Sometimes it can take up to a year for an online application to get reviewed because of the volume of applications a company may receive. It doesn't mean you can't find a job before then; just don't expect an immediate response.

Since the advent of technology, the internet is probably where you'll find the most and the best opportunities. You may want to check out the *Forbes* magazine article written by Jacqueline Smith entitled "The Top 100 Websites for Your Career."[1] Since we spend an average of 79 percent of our waking hours online anyway, these sites will give you plenty to research.

---

1 Jacqueline Smith, "The Top 100 Websites for Your Career," www.forbes.com, 9/18/2013.

Mentally Condition Yourself to Action

This is a sample of a reasonable schedule to give yourself the mental conditioning to keep looking when you're not getting responses.

Determine several important things that will be accomplished that day.	
8:30 a.m.–10:00 a.m.	Get up, dress, and let's begin—suit and tie not required
10:30 a.m.–12:00 p.m.	Online research, tweet
12:30 p.m.–3:00 p.m.	Work on résumé and web search, tweet
3:15 p.m.–5:00 p.m.	Personal break—eat, tweet
Miscellaneous	Bathroom break – tweet–simultaneous!
7:00 p.m.–8:00p.m.	Facebook connections, tweeting, dinner, etc.

I can imagine what you're thinking. "So am I supposed to do the same thing every day until I find a job?" Of course not. The point is to get you in the habit of using your mind, body, intellect, skills, and technology to do something other than texting (without a purpose), sitting at home, and watching TV until the "job fairy" comes a knockin' at your door.

Okay, have a sense of humor! You see my point, right? Just make a schedule that gets you moving, thinking, and most importantly, producing results. Since you have already mastered using your technology, use it as a weapon to your benefit. For example, many of us have a hundred or more connections on our Facebook page—why not throw out the call for job opportunities? You have a better shot, because these are not just friends; they are also acquaintances, previous coworkers, and even past employers.

Now that you have a schedule, let's look at a method you can use to follow along with the process. Remember in the process of seeking a job, I can almost guarantee that you won't remember the number of résumés you've sent, all of the applications you've completed, the information you've downloaded, or the networking websites you've joined. This is why it's best to have a systematic approach and this mini-spreadsheet can help with the process.

JOB SEARCH PROSPECTS AND OPPORTUNITIES

Company	Job Title	Salary	Email	Phone	Resp
ABC, Inc.	Administrative Executive	$46,000.00	mjm@yahoo.com	xxx-xxxx	No
Acme Eng.	Engineer	$98.000.00	acme@ack.com	xxx-xxxx	No
EFG, Mfg	Camera Operator	$39,000.00	dvdvideo@.com	xxx-xxxx	Yes
HIJ Heating	Heating Repair	$32,000.00	HIJ@klmn.com	xxx-xxxx	No

Wow, you've done quite a bit of work there. Congratulations! Well, don't celebrate just yet. Now that you've determined your vision, set your direction, prepared a plan of action, our next chapter will evaluate the types of industries that suit your skills, abilities, and personality best. After all, if technology is not your strongest skill, then working at Best Buy probably wouldn't work for you.

FYI, the positions posted above are not active positions and the companies don't even exist!

CHAPTER 5

RECOGNIZING YOUR MARKETABLE SKILLS

Your marketable skills are the reason employer's will select you over someone else. Finding employment begins with the skills you already have in conjunction with your talents and education. What I mean is your talent is an aptitude, gift, knack or ability that comes naturally or without effort. As you review this list of marketable skills, look also at the items on the list that come naturally to you. Whether it's auto repair, hair stylist, or clothing design, the ideal job should involve both so you can use them in creating or building a career.

Place a check mark next to those areas in which you actually have experience. If possible, select at least four occupations or skills that you have experience or are pursuing. As mentioned earlier, it's important to understand that every job you have may not allow you to do everything you love. Each position should be a learning experience. If not, you'll get bored quickly and will probably quit. But no matter what your occupation these four components are a *requirement* no matter what your job.

For inspiration, look at this list of people who utilized these four critical skills that paid off in developing their careers – before they became famous:

♦ Morgan Freeman was in television on *The Electric Company,* a children's educational show.
♦ Angelina Jolie was a funeral director.

◆ Randy Jackson's first job was a grocery bagger.

◆ Brad Pitt's first job was wearing a chicken suit for a chicken restaurant franchise.

◆ Tom Cruise's first job was a paperboy.

◆ Jennifer Aniston was a telemarketer and waitress.

◆ Jennifer Lopez was a "Flygirl" or dancer on the comedy show *In Living Color.*

◆ Matthew McConaughey cleaned chicken coops and washed dishes.

Though their first jobs started at the bottom, the four D's have taken them to the TOP!

dreams, drive, determination, and destiny

Marketable Skills

__Accountant/Auditor
__Actor/Actress
__Administrative Asst.
__Advertising
__Airline Pilot
__Animal Care
__Architecture
__Auto Repair
__Banking Industry
__Barber
__Bartender
__Bookkeeper
__Building Inspector
__Bus Driver
__Butcher/Meat Cutter
__Buyer
__Cabinet Installation
__Cable Installer

__Cable Repair Asst.
__Car Sales
__Carpet Installer
__Case Manager
__Cashier
__Chef Cook
__Chemical Engineer
__Child Care Specialist
__Computer Analyst
__Construction
__Custodian
__Data Entry
__Dental Assistant
__Dental Hygienist
__Dentist
__Dispatcher
__Drafter

__Drywall Installer
__Economist
__Editor

__Electrical Technician
__Employment
   Specialist
__Engineer
__Farmer
__Film Maker
__Finance Manager
__Firefighter
__Food Counter Worker
__Groundskeeper
__Guard
__Hairdresser
__Health and Fitness
__Health Care Aide
__Hotel Clerk
__Housekeeper
__Kitchen Worker
__Lawyer
__Legal Assistant
__Machinist Attendant
__Mail Carrier Industry
__Mailroom Clerk
__Mechanical Engineer
__Mental Health
   Specialist
__Messenger
__Minister
__Mover
__Musician
__News Reporter
__LPN/Nurse
__Nurse's Aide Buyer
__Order Clerk

__Painter
__Pastor
__Pharmacist
__Photographer
__Physical Therapist
__Plumber
__Police Officer
__Postal Worker
__Press Operator
__Printer
__Production Worker
__Psychologist
__Real Estate Agent
__Receptionist
__Roofer
__Sales Retail
__Sanitation Worker
__Security Guard
__Social Worker
__Surveyor
__Taxi Driver
__Teacher
__Technician
__Telemarketer
__Television Editor
__Trainer
__Truck Driver Manager
__Underwriter
__Upholsterer
__Video Producer
__Wait Staff
__Water/Sewage
__Welder
__Writer

Critical Job Skills

On top of the skills listed above and regardless of the formal training or experience you have in a specific career, there are four skills that everyone needs to have to be successful in any career. From the moment you sit down for the interview, your communication skills require that you advocate for yourself concerning the job. Each of these qualities support you in a number of areas so don't take them lightly. As we move through the book, I will elaborate in how to utilize each of these critical skills, where you can find them and how to *master* them.

**Four Critical Skills
Every Employer Wants**

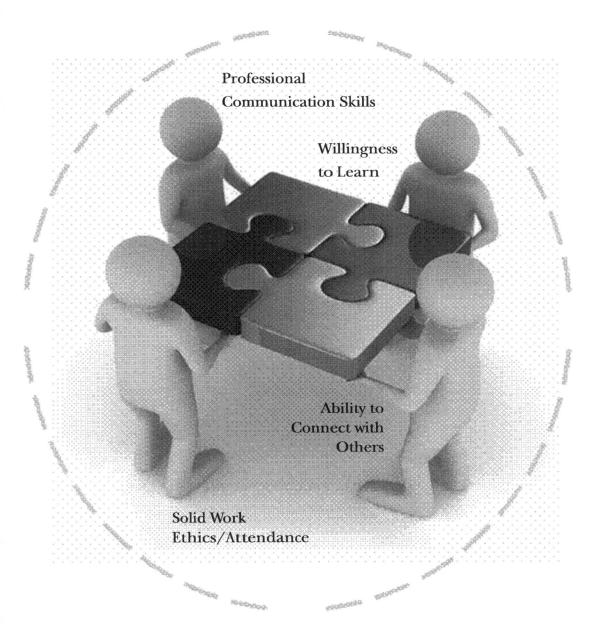

Professional
Communication Skills

Willingness
to Learn

Ability to
Connect with
Others

Solid Work
Ethics/Attendance

CHAPTER 6

WHAT TO DO WITH THOSE OLD BUSINESS CARDS

Have you ever looked through your stash of business cards? Do you think you would remember the person on the card if you saw him or her? Probably not. But here's where thinking outside of the box comes in handy folks. Each card has the name of a company and a representative. At some point, there was a reason to exchange cards in the first place. This is where you can do some research and find out more about the company. It's also a great way to a) try to reconnect with people you've met previously, and b) find out if the company may have job opportunities.

By the way, there *is* a technique to asking for and receiving a business card as well. First, at some point in the conversation, you should mention, "I'd like to contact you again to discuss this when we have a little more time. Do you have a card with you?"

This way it becomes a mutual exchange. If they offer you a card, hold the card as if it's a diamond, look at the card, and read it out loud. Yes, I said *out loud*. First, it allows the name and information to sink into your brain. Second, it makes people feel important when you say their names out loud. It also extends the conversation and it turns the discussion into a personal interaction.

If there is very specific information to remember, let the person know by saying something like this: "This is great."

So, now that you have all of these business cards, old and new, how can you use them to your advantage? Go to the LinkedIn site to find out if the person on the card is still with that particular organization. Just to give you a little more insight, *LinkedIn* is a professional online networking site which allows you to reach out to previous colleagues, potential employers, and friends who are seeking employment. Unlike Facebook, this site is utilized as a professional online résumé – which means using only a professional headshot and work experience. According to Susan Adams, a Forbes staffing member, LinkedIn is a decade old and has more than 200 million members. " www.forbes.com

Just as you would present yourself for a physical interview, the concept is the same. Anything you would not present to an employer in an interview, you don't list here.

Example: photos of yourself in a casual environment, your personal plans for the weekend, what you ate the night before or your upcoming class reunion.

You will need to create a professional profile of course, but the fact that you are now "friends" gives you a reason to reconnect again. People have asked me, "Do you really need business cards now that you can put the information online?" That may be true, but people still use cards as a primary connector and that's why you should too. Think of it as a mini-résumé. Vistaprint is the site to help you with the process of producing your very own card. It also offers a vast array of styles and designs you can utilize to give it the right professional edge and the pricing is more than affordable. Just go online and take a look.

Well, what should you put on your business card if you are not currently employed? I'm glad you asked. Below is what I'd like to call a mini-résumé.

Marcus Whitley

Specializing in Home Repairs

Painting   Electrician
Drywalls   Roofing
Gutter Cleaning   Window Replacement

We are the manpower to make it happen!

Always give people three business cards: one to keep, one to lose, and one to give to someone who might need your services.

Below is a sample note written to reconnect with someone thru a LinkedIn connection or a business card. You can also use this as a basic template of which you can tailor.

Kimberly A. Winner

6461 Staples Drive * Plato, TX 78910 * (913) 123-4567

August 17, 2019

Hello Angela Freedman:

Thank you for connecting with me on the LinkedIn network. I recently ran across your card and was going to reach out to you. We spoke at the Restaurant Management conference last year. Are you still with Blessings and Barbeque? If you get a few moments this week, I'd like to catch up. My number is (913) 123-4567.

Thanks.

Kimberly

Keep the note comfortable, in a casual but professional style. Just make sure to ask to connect with the person.

CHAPTER 7

SO WHAT COLOR *IS* YOUR PARACHUTE?

A re you familiar with the book *What Color Is Your Parachute?*[2] What do you mean, you haven't heard of it? Stop what you're doing, and go buy this book or get it on Kindle. This book has sold over six million copies around the world. What makes the book unique is that it deals with the psychology of finding a job as well as understanding the components of what we go through in the process physically, mentally, and emotionally. But wait—finish my book first!

Below is a list of websites that test your personality and abilities to work in various occupations and industries. Let me say that there are many other online tests out there, but I have found the five listed here to be the most effective because they compare your occupational aptitude to all jobs in the world. They often request that you type in your zip code so that they can better target your

Career Quiz and Assessment	http://www.careertest.us
Myers-Briggs Complete Personality Job Assessment	https://www.mbticomplete.com
Department of Labor's Career Center	http://www.onetonline.org/
Career Online Profile	http://www.futureproofyourcareer.com
Skill Cow	http://www.skillcow.com

---

2 Richard Nelson Bolles, *What Color Is Your Parachute?*, (Berkley, CA: Ten Speed Press, 2002).

city and your industry to help you to identify which position most likely will yield success. You're not required to take them all. But I would recommend you use one of the tests and master the system and use the others as a resource. Of course it's up to you, but I *am* the expert.

Ms. Dawn Rosenberg McKay is an expert in career development and a member of the National Career Development Association (NCDA). Her blog http://www.careerplanning.about.com offers great articles with insight and information in career planning. The test on the website is a personal assessment of your career interests and then offers you a report card to help you determine if it's the right career for you. (Cool, right?)

I'll be honest; I was a little skeptical about these tests and whether they were really accurate. However, after I took a test on monster.com, "Discover Your Perfect Career Quiz," I was surprised at how accurate it was and what it revealed.

One of the tests listed is the Myers-Briggs Job Assessment. Have you ever heard of it? The Myers-Briggs Personality Job Assessment Type is a list of questions that determine your natural personality strengths, weaknesses and areas that would allow you to excel in a particular field or industry. For example, if you were to score extremely high in handling numbers, it would evaluate a listing of occupations in which those traits would be successful. Occupations which carry the greatest opportunity for success would be . . . . .

- ◆ Money market broker
- ◆ finance manager
- ◆ fiscal officer
- ◆ accountant
- ◆ bookkeeper
- ◆ controller
- ◆ business
- ◆ CPA

So, the Myers Briggs test is broken into four basic personality components:

Extrovert an outgoing, gregarious person. A person concerned primarily with the physical and social environment

Introvert a private and shy person. A person concern primarily with his or her own internal thoughts and feelings

Intuitive perceiving by, as a person or the mind resulting from, or involving intuition *knowledge.*

Perceiver to recognize, discern, envision, or understand: I perceive a note of sarcasm in your voice. This is a nice idea but I perceive difficulties in putting it into practice.

After taking the test myself, the results of the test were very telling and extremely accurate. My test determined that I was an 'ENFP'. In plain English, this means my personality is *(E) Extrovert (N) Intuitive (F) Feeler,* and *(P) Perceiver.* My personality is one that works most effectively with people and thrives in an occupation with lots of people interaction. The intuitive label means that I'm not inclined to utilize my analytical skills—I have none! My intuition skills are strong and internal and seem to be most effective when I use them as a tool. The test also indicated that I'm a feeler. My work habits are based on my emotional compass or the feelings of others. Yes, I'm very sensitive and emotionally involved—not just with the work, but the outcome as well. And perceiver means to interpret underlying emotions.

Keep in mind that the Myers-Briggs Indicator Test is not the only personality-style system that exists for the purpose of determining your natural personality traits; it is one of many. Other personality assessors include one known as *DiSC Personality Types – meaning* **D**ominance, **I**nfluence, **S**teadiness and **C**onscientiousness. *Jung, True Colors, Hippocrates and even Dr. Phil* has one!

So, the test determined that the occupations listed which would offer me the highest levels of success would be:

- ♦ artist
- ♦ *advertising account executive*
- ♦ *career/outplacement counselor*
- ♦ copywriter
- ♦ *corporate team trainer*
- ♦ developer of educational software
- ♦ *graphic designer*
- ♦ *human resources professional*
- ♦ *inventor*
- ♦ journalist/magazine reporter
- ♦ *management consultant*
- ♦ psychologist

Interestingly enough, at some point in my career, I have held seven out of the twelve suggested positions. I believe that every position I have ever had has brought me to my life's work as a professional speaker and trainer. Many of my activities fall in line with those skills—teaching, tutoring, job/career coaching, producing DVDs, books, online courses, and marketing, working in sales, and finally, motivational speaking. After doing some true soul-searching, I came to understand my calling *"Empowering Others to Find Their Destiny!"*

One final online test I recommend is the Future Proof Your Career test at www.futureproofyourcareer.com/?hop=grooveit.

This test allows you to determine your top three fields of work selected from the official US Department of Labor careers database on the basis of your individual responses to the questionnaire. It tells you:

♦ Which one of the sixteen career personality types you fit into and what types of work you are best suited to do.

♦ Your six dominant career abilities and three dominant career intelligences. Again, this provides clues to your most suitable career. Pay particular attention to how you rate on the six key skills of the "Knowledge Age."[3]

---

3 Richard Calking and Tania Dally, "Authentic Direction,"Career Mentoring Institute, 2009. www. futureproofyourcareer.com.

PROFESSIONAL ACTION PLAN
Now that you know, how will you grow?

I have designed this page to give you the opportunity to determine what valuable information you have received and how you can implement strategies discussed in each chapter.

1. _____

2. _____

3. _____

4. _____

5. _____

6. _____

THE JOB MARKET IS GROWING

What! Where? I know. I didn't believe it either. Maybe you can't see it if you're unemployed, underemployed, or only working part-time, but according to the Bureau of Labor Statistics or the 'BLS' it says quite the opposite.

The Bureau of Labor Statistics is a unit of the United States Department of Labor. The BLS is a governmental statistical agency that collects, processes, analyzes, and disseminates essential statistical data to the American public, the U.S. Congress, other Federal agencies, State and local governments, business, and labor representatives concerning the employment statistics around the country. They conduct research into how much families need to earn to be able to enjoy a decent standard of living. They keep track month-to-month on the number of positions created, those transitioned, terminated, part-time, and any other position which yields a wage. The key is to understand timing, location, industry and where they are hiding.

Okay, I'm gonna' let you in on a little secret. I recently found an online series known as Mom Corps at www.momcorps.com. This website offers a Weekly Hot Jobs Listing. Initially, I thought it was only for mothers only obviously because of the name. To my complete surprise, Mom Corps is a staffing company that does weekly notifications of current job listing from Chicago to Puerto Rico to Canada. The strategy here is to research the companies and then find one of them in your neck of the woods. Go ahead and take a peek yourself. If you get nothing else out of this book, I'm absolutely sure this is all you need. You can put the book down. Hold on; I was just kidding. There's more to come.

Are they real jobs? Absolutely. Over the past six months I've begun to notice that Mom Corps is listing virtual jobs as well. The company may not specifically target your area of expertise on any given week, but I think it's always worth looking into. They offer everything from full-time jobs to virtual positions – which is the new 'work-from-home' concept.

Exploring Every Option

Your job search can take many different avenues. By the time most people have exhausted their online efforts, they have forgotten some of the basic strategies that existed before the technology age. These are the options I have found to be most effective in the job-seeking arena.

The following are employment resources readily available in your community that are often free:

♦ club memberships
♦ college placement guides
♦ former coworkers/clients
♦ government job listings
♦ internship connections
♦ job fair opportunities
♦ local community organizations
♦ library access
♦ newspaper want ads
♦ networking groups

♦ private employment agencies
♦ sorority/fraternity connections
♦ state employment agencies
♦ temporary agencies

I can here you now saying, 'well, I've tried so of these and I didn't find anything.' You may not find the right position the first three times to use these avenues. On the average, It takes seven 'no's to get one 'yes'. Here's the key – *You Only Need One Yes* to take care of your family.

So are you gonna get on it this time or what? Make sure your résumé is tight and go for it!

PART 2

Building A Professional Image On Paper With Your Cover Letter

Do I Need a Cover Letter?

Absolutely! A cover letter is the handshake before the actual interview. Consider this: have you ever met someone at a party who didn't tell you his or her name and some additional information? Of course not. You're asking for a job; you'd better do so with a professional standard. The cover letter is one of the tools required in introducing yourself. The person on the receiving end wants to know something about you over and above your résumé; your writing skills to be most important. Think of your cover letter as your professional introduction.

Five Key Qualities of a STAND-OUT Cover Letter

- Be yourself. Your personality shows through in your writing. If you've got a sense of humor, use it.
- Explain how you found out about the position: If you connected online, let the employer know. It's a question I'm sure your interviewer will ask, because if you found the position online, your prospective employers need to know which site you found it on, and they need to know how useful it was.
- Document information related to the position itself. I suggest you utilize the exact terminology used in the job ad. Keep it simple. If the job ad asks for someone with lots of sales experience, consider saying something like: "I believe my sales experience as a sales director at my previous position could be a huge benefit to this position. In my former role, I managed a $500,000 budget."
- Mention what excites you about the position. This lets the employer know you have a genuine interest.
- Make sure all of the information listed on your résumé and cover letter is current. You'd be shocked at how often people forget something important like a contact number.

Below I have designed a number of cover letters to use as samples. Of course each has its' own style.

> *Push for the Interview.*
> *This is where your marketing skills really count!*

CHRIS THOMPSON
18502 Stuart Hall Road, Falls Church, VA 22042, (222) 567-8910
Cthompson@gmail.com

Ms. Anna Stapleton
Director of Employment Services
Brooklyn Health System
2990 Teller Court, Suite 100
New York, NY 20002

RE: Clerical Services Position (4262) or Medical Records Position (4995) Human Resource Director	**(Make it clear which positions you are applying for)** **(Use the position title rather than 'whom it may concern')**
Dear Ms. Stapleton:	**(Use the designation of Mr. or Ms. which is formal)**

I recently looked on **the INOVA.com website** and saw many openings for which I am qualified.

What I liked about these positions is that they offer opportunities to serve others while enhancing my skills. I'd love to be able to put my skills into action regardless of whether it's the clerical position or medical records. My résumé is attached.

In my current position, my major responsibilities involve extensive customer contact and ensuring customer satisfaction. This, combined with my clerical skills and experience, makes me an ideal fit for the medical office environment.

My personal attributes include consistency in performance, willingness to learn new skills, and flexibility. Each helps me to excel with my talents. I noticed your ad required a flexible schedule, and that is another reason this position would be a good fit. **I am currently enrolled in several college** courses.

I would be happy to schedule an interview this coming week. **My number is (222) 567-8910.** Thank you in advance, Ms. Stapleton, and I look forward to hearing from you and **becoming a part of the INOVA team**.

Chris Thompson

- ◆ **How did you hear about the position**
- ◆ **What you are currently doing (looking, transitioning, moving)**
- ◆ **The skills, knowledge, and experience you bring to the organization**
- ◆ **A phone number or how you can be reached**
- ◆ **Don't forget to ask for the job!**

Career Building

Helen E. Carpenter
6295 Minniville Avenue
New York, NY 105508
Mobile 718-793-7487 or Home 718-747-8976

June 25, 2018

Dear Human Resource Manager:

I am pleased to submit my information for your consideration for the executive director position. After reviewing the job description, I know that my nonprofit management and fundraising experience would be a perfect fit for your division. I have a wealth of experience as an executive director for nonprofits with areas of specialty in both management and fundraising. In addition, I am proud to say that my grant development acquisitions have led to a combined $26 million increase in funding for several organizations. I'm confident that these efforts, combined with my existing funding contacts, would qualify me as an excellent candidate for this position.

My résumé, along with my writing sample, and letters of recommendation from a former client are attached. Realizing that a brief written biography cannot totally describe my skills and personality, I welcome the opportunity for an interview so I might come to know your needs and work together toward success.

Sincerely,

Helen E. Carpenter
Attachment

Phyllis Winder

354   Clouds Avenue * Fort Knox, KY 89101 * (C) 989-720-1972 * pwinder@yahoo.com

August 19, 2018

POSITION TITLE: HUMAN RESOURCES MANAGEMENT
Chicago Division: Area RPG: 69694

HR Director:

I am replying to your notice for the position of a human resource director in your Chicago division. I was pleasantly surprised because I am a native of Chicago. My experience emphasizes both government agencies and non-profit. My ten year membership of the (SHRM) Society of Human Resource Management gives me unique perspective in managing this division.

My greatest assets include my communication skills, flexibility, and the ability to collaborate effectively between staff and management. I know one thing without exception is that the success of a company comes from the value of its people.

I will be visiting with my parents over the next two weeks and would love an opportunity to discuss how I can be of value within your Chicago division. I can be reached at 989-720-1972 and I look forward to your call.

Sincerely,

Phyllis Winder

How Important Is Your E-Mail Address

Does your e-mail address make a difference to an employer? You bet your, um, bottom dollar it does! I read an article online some time ago written by Rick Sherrille entitled "Your E-mail Address Is INCREDIBLE...and That's Not a Compliment," and it got my attention right away. The article focused on the impact of your e-mail address.

Most people have more than one e-mail address, right? If you only have one, you should probably create another. Why? It's as simple as separating your personal life from your professional life. Using your name is easiest for someone to remember. Consider that the résumé begins with your name and address. Next is the e-mail address. You are advertising yourself as a professional, so your e-mail address and all correspondence should reinforce that idea. So if you see an e-mail from shelleysexy10@aol.com (fictitious), what is your first impression? I can tell you that even if you were to interview Shelley, the lasting impression of her address would probably leave a negative imprint. Don't get me wrong. If it's your personal address, feel free to express yourself. You just don't want to lose your credibility in the process.

Believe it or not, people do put a lot of stock in your choice of e-mail and web addresses. Often people really haven't considered the impact—or imprint, I should say—that their address will have on the HR director. For example, since my area of expertise is employment, my e-mail address is info@theemployment-lady.com. Simple, right? Basic rules apply when it comes to a professional image. I have spoken with hiring director's who told me about address that would drop your bottom lip. Of course, based on confidentiality, I am unable to disclose any – *oh, but some them were good!* The question to ask yourself when you send your résumé or other credentials is this: does my e-mail address represent a professional image? Or does it show people that I can't be taken seriously? I guess that depends on what type of image you'd like to project.

PART 3

How to Create A Unique Résumé That Fits You

CHAPTER 11

WHAT YOUR RÉSUMÉ SAYS ABOUT YOU!

If you want potential employers to take you seriously, you must have three building tools before you begin. These include:

- your cover letter—the schematics and foundation
- your résumé, otherwise known as a curriculum vitae—the building blocks and construction
- your references—the career job inspectors

The interview is the callback for the final inspection; accepting the position is the completion; and your first paycheck is a ribbon-cutting celebration!

Résumés are not optional—they are mandatory in most cases! In some industries, applications are requested instead of résumés. All companies are now required to have something on file that shows your employment history—even if it has nothing to do with the position. Today, you can use software to produce a résumé at the touch of a button. Keep in mind that once you hit the "send" button, you cannot be assured of the document's format, whether or not your prospective employer receives it, or even whether anyone reads it. That's why sending a hard copy is a nice backup strategy (when it's possible, of course).

While it may seem like common sense, your name, address, phone number, and e-mail address must be on your résumé as well. The information needs to be the most current at that time. So, if you recently got married, your married name should be listed. Imagine what it says to the employer if you tell someone in the interview, 'Sorry, that was my old name. I got married four months ago.' I can say this with the upmost confidence - even if you don't get the job, I promise you the person will remember the fact that you couldn't take the time to change it on your résumé. And *NEVER*, I mean *NEVER* scratch out information either. Scratching out information is just plain lazy and diminishes your professionalism. Simply let the person know you will send an updated version of your information.

Another key component people don't often put down is a list of hobbies. I know, it may not seem like much, but I promise you if you have a common interest with the person reading your résumé, it will make him or her sit up. Whenever I included my military background, it immediately established a connection with people who either served in the military or who have a friend or family member who do.

What they understand is that my background already has strengths and characteristics of what they can see as valuable. So remember to leave some room to list a few hobbies. Example: marathon running, scuba diving, reading, skiing or advocating for the homeless. Of these hobbies listed, what would pull your interest for discussion?

Also consider something that shows advantage to the employer, i.e. your ability to speak multiple languages, CPR, safety or driving certifications, and even volunteer activities. It shows you have a heart to give and work within the community. But *never* include details which could offer the possibility of discrimination.

The standard résumé length should be no more than two pages (on average). Hold on…take it easy. I didn't say it could *only* be two pages. That's a misconception. What must be considered first is your occupation. Those with careers that encompass various doctorates, medical, psychiatry or legal expertise, and other positions. Some curricula vitae can run as long as five pages when it lists doctorate information or books and television appearances and published magazine articles. It's also important to consider how much time most people have to read résumés that are in their online inboxes. Your résumé must be sharp enough to pull the person's interest, and valuable enough to keep it.

What if I don't have a stellar work history?

As I said previously, there is no such thing as one style fits all résumé. With that in mind, you will need to use a two-prong approach to submitting your résumé. First, the font size will need to be larger than the normal 12 font style. This would require that you use a 13 font approach in that it is larger than the usual, but it offers a style that doesn't stand out to the point of the obvious. Here's what I mean:

Larry G. Tarry
This font style is called 'Book Antiqua' size 13 font

This is a basic platform to using font styles that are simple and easy to read such as 'Time New Romans.' My book is written in this font. However, there are a listing of fonts in any software (in the upper left-hand corner) that are usable as well. First, determine the type of job you are applying for. For example: If you are designating something as a signature, you may use a 'Mistral' font *like this*: *which has a handwritten feel.*

This résumé sample is presented on page 48 to show a reflection of designing your résumé in light of the gaps in employment.

Résumé Designs That Work!

After three weeks, nine hours, and twenty-five minutes, you've finally completed your résumé. Then a friend takes a look at it and says, "I would take that out." Then you show it to someone else who says, "I think you should add that back in." The more people you show it to, the more suggestions you will receive so don't pass it around like M&M's. Give it to someone who reviews résumés before uploading it to an employer's website. (your best friend doesn't count) Make sure you give yourself some dedicated time and effort to develop it. It *may take* three weeks, nine hours, and twenty-five minutes. The energy you put into preparing it, is also a reflection in the type of work you will do upon getting the job as well. Understand, no two résumés will look the same so never try and compare yours against someone else's. However, you may duplicate areas of someone's résumé that will offer some punch to yours.

Designing your résumé is just as important as the information on it! The basic protocol is to capitalize and **bold information** in both the Titles of the positions and Descriptions of the position. The point is to make the information to stand out and more importantly to make it as easy as possible for the reader. That's why spacing makes a dramatic difference as well.

Consider that most people read in bullets and colors, use areas of your résumés to add both. Using the *'USAToday'* is your greatest example. The format of the article is what leads you into the story. So, your résumés format is most crucial. The newspaper editors actually design the paper for an easy read using color, underlines, boxes and other strategies to focus your attention on various articles. Use the top of the résumé as your headline. From your name to the personal biography or objective. Develop what I'd like to call a 'Professional Profile'. This will allow you to focus on your experience rather than the number of years. Tailor your experience toward the requirements of the position itself. It's not necessary that you change the entire résumé each time you apply for a different position, but it needs to be tailored. Since companies are using scanning resources to input the documents they receive, this is where something known as 'keywords' come in. If you are applying for a position related to driving, some of the key words might include: transportation, certification, trucks, vehicles, passengers, etc. By the way, even though my focus has been related to résumés, these suggestions also apply to applications as well.

You are the 'brand'. A brand is the identification of the product and its' benefits – like a commercial. Each product has its own brand. When you hear the name *'Tide'* you think of clothes. If you hear the name *'Ford'* you think trucks.

'Crest', you think toothpaste. You want to become the brand for your résumés. Marja Lee *'The Employment Lady'*.   Feel free to use the different font options **_available_** without making it too intrusive.

On the following pages, you will notice several résumé designs for a variety of work environments – from high school to those with disadvantaged backgrounds. Remember, your résumé represents not only your experience, but more importantly your value!

(The names and data are for fictitious people, places, addresses, phone numbers, and email addresses, so please don't try to contact these people for jobs or dates.)

LORI FRIEDMAN

<u>**2600 Holiday Drive, Columbus, OH 43210, 614-444-0000,**</u>

<u>**lorifriedman@gmail.com**</u>

(High School Résumé)

Personal Life's Goal: To pursue a law degree from Georgetown University.

<u>**Extracurricular Activities**</u>

Zeta Phi Beta Sorority	Sept. 2019 – Present
1 Hr. week	Grade 11
Auxillary service and scholarship organization	

Gartland Afterschool Program	Grades 9-11
Reference Ms. Angela Anderson, Program Director	

<u>**Volunteer for Community Services**</u>

Food Distribution	May 2018
Mentoring with elderly	
Total Hours: 2	
I helped distribute food to the elderly with disabilities	

Helped at Eye Doctor	March 2018
Clear Vision Express	Grade 9
Total Hours: 23	
I helped out the receptionist and helped the manager process the insurance checks.	

Translator	February 2018
Collaborations Community School	Grade 9
Total Hours: 12	
Translated at parent/teacher conferences.	

Selling Chocolates	November 2018
Anderson High School-Minnie Howard Campus	Grade 9
Total Hours: 12	
I was selling Chocolates for Valentine's Day during lunch periods.	

Gift Wrapping	October 2018
Barnes & Noble	Grade 8
Total Hours: 4	
Holiday gift wrapped for the clients.	

Reading: Total Hours: 3	Sept. 2018
Read to the kids in Spanish and in 9th grade read Halloween books.	Grade 8

TERRY A. THOMPKINS

4737 42nd Street, Queens, NY 27880 Apt. 437, 577-222-4737, tat@yahoo.com

(Terms underlined are power words)

POSITION TITLE: VAN DRIVER

Extensive experience in the area of transporting individuals with physical as well as mental disabilities. Demonstrates sensitivity, sound judgment, and a strong knowledge of safety procedures as it pertains to performing the tasks I love most – driving and working with people

(Date of experience not listed as it's too far back)
(Requirements listed based on client's needs.)

TRANSPORTATION EXPERIENCE

→ Perfect driving record for the past six years
→ CPR and first-aid certified
→ Experience in using a 7-passenger van
→ Able to operate wheelchair lifts
→ Understands the purpose of vehicle maintenance and safety requirements
→ Able to make passengers feel secure and safe
→ Has passed course in handling difficult behavior of passengers with disabilities

(Date listed on the left not the far right because there is no current work experience.)

Senior Services Community Center
Head Cook and Staff Support – 2009

→ Prepared and served food for clients at the senior residents.
→ Monitored sanitation practices to ensure that employees follow standards and regulations.
→ Determined the quantity and quality of food.
→ Demonstrated new cooking techniques and equipment to staff.

Safeway
Sales Associate and Cashier- 1999

→ Maintained stock control records on all supply items. Set up and design merchandise displays for promotion and sales.
→ Reconciled cash and credit purchases and resolved any discrepancies.
→ Showed genuine concern to ensure that the store maintained a professional standard.

VOLUNTEER WORK

→ House of Mercy Thrift Store
→ Youth Prevention Program

(Always list volunteer work regardless of how far back (List any community programs ex-offenders currently participate.)

STEVEN B. JACKSON, JR.
32332 Sandavall Boulevard, Sacramento, CA 76543
Home: 949-212-2000, Cell: 888-555-7869   E-mail: stevtheman@verizon.net

---

PROFILE
Executive Director with extensive experience in broad-based management advisory experience within the government and private sectors. With a performance-driven and market-driven attitude, my organization has done exceptional work in handling challenging program changes and improving environments. Outstanding communication, negotiation, and team-building skills. Recognized for a commitment to excellence in staff management.

Areas of Expertise

• Project Management	• Marketing	• Counseling	• Advocacy
• Negotiation Skills	• Medicare Expertise	• Team Building	• Research

---

Sacramento Agency On Aging, Sacramento, CA
Program Manager, Healthcare and Assistance Program   9/2017–7/2025
Certified Volunteer Counselor

- Directed a county-wide Medicare advocacy, education, and counseling program for beneficiaries, families, and caregivers.
- Served as one of two agency focal points on all aspects of the senior executive service, including pay, leave, retirement, classification, and appointment.
- Partnered with national health care advocacy organization to provide in-kind resources.
- Delivered series of well-received presentations to professional groups, service providers, and community groups regarding specific aspects of the Medicareprogram.

Government Employees Health Association, Sacramento, CA
Senior Account Executive, Healthcare and Assistance Program   9/2010-2/2016

- Served as main speaker at company's first webcast seminar.
- Top producing account executive for four consecutive years and rated highest for customer satisfaction in federal agency polls.

STEVEN B. JACKSON, JR.

Government Employees Health Association, Sacramento, CA

Senior Account Executive, Healthcare and Assistance Program   9/2010-2/2016

- Solely established company's northeastern market, generating a lucrative customer base in a previously unexplored territory.
- Increased company's presence at open-season enrollment events and conferences.
- Provided coaching in sales and marketing techniques throughout the country.

Department of Justice (DOJ), Criminal Division

Human Resource (HR) Specialist   6/2006–6/2007

- Researched content for preliminary design of an executive resources home page.
- Acted as Executive Secretary on various departmental performance and selection boards.
- Assisted with the implementation of the first SES pay-for-performance change in executive compensation.
- Interacted with key officials in the Justice Department, the Office of the Assistant Attorney General, and White House Liaison on political appointments, reassignments, and promotions.
- Shortened cycle for filling critical executive vacancies to 30 days or less.
- Developed new position descriptions and comprehensive evaluation statements for each of the division's 38 senior executive positions.
- Authored presidential rank and incentive award nominations for top senior officials.

MARCUS A. CHANDELER
1431 South Columbus St, Alexandria, VA 22314   mcatlas@yahoo.com (703) 254-9607

SKILLS and QUALIFICATIONS

Over ten years of hands-on experience supervising, managing and maintaining apartment grounds and senior living facilities. Certifications in the following: HVAC repair, water heaters, landscaping, painting, plumbing, roofing. Currently serves on a contract basis for temporary services and repairs.

PROFESSIONAL EXPERIENCE

2020–2024   **MASTERCRAFT INTERIORS**   **Columbus, OH**
                              Senior Maintenance Engineer

Served as supervisor and overseer of an engineering staff of five senior engineers for an apartment complex of 185 units. Responsible for hiring, scheduling, conducted performance reviews, reprimands and/or terminations. Scheduled staff for certifications and testing required by state housing commission.

2016–2020   **FOSTER MANAGEMENT APARTMENTS**   **Columbus, OH**
                              Maintenance Supervisor

Directed the operation, preventive repairs and installation of all heating, air conditioning, refrigeration equipment throughout the complex. Ensured all required requisitions and documentation were completed. Trained all new hires in safety requirements.

2014-2016   **RICHARDSON'S APARTMENTS**   **Toledo, OH**
                              Maintenance worker

Maintained interior and exterior upkeep of the 150 unit apartments. Performed all other duties outlined in the company's preventative maintenance handbook, including adherence to the work order process. Experienced in drywall, painting, and basic repairs and landscaping of the property.

2009-2014   **INDEPENDENT CONTRACTOR FOR PRIVATE HOME REPAIRS**

(Provided services on a contract basis through private and government funded positions.)
(This notation explains that you have worked sporadically, but not a fulltime position.)

HOBBIES: Volunteers for the youth program for ministry, running and reading.

RÉSUMÉ DESIGN SAMPLE WITHIN THE FOOD SERVICE INDUSTRY

Summary of Qualifications

- Extensive experience working in variety of positions within the food service industry.
- Responsible for supervision, planning, developing and monitoring all operational activities.
- Collaborated with registered dietitian to ensure proper nutritional needs of residents.
- Trained in Quality Assurance measurements, therapeutic diets and health code regulations.

Professional Experience

Grand canyon nursing facility   2017- 2022
Food service specialist

- Monitored food preparation methods, portion sizes and garnishing presentation of food to ensure that food is prepared and presented in an acceptable manner.
- Managed a staff of 19 in food service department which entailed performance appraisals.
- Disciplinary actions, and tracking and recording personnel leave.
- Recruited and hired staff, including cooks and other kitchen workers.
- Determined work schedules to meet the needs of the department.
- Coordinated planning, budgeting, and purchasing for all the food operations within nursing facility.
- Estimated amounts and costs of required supplies, such as food and ingredients.
- Inspected supplies, equipment, and work areas to ensure conformance to established standards.
- Trained all staff in the kitchen maintenance, preparation, cooking, garnishing and presentation of food.
- Collaborated with other personnel to plan and develop recipes and menus, taking into account the residents dietary needs.

Senior living nursing & rehabilitation center   2012-2015
Head cook

- Check the quality of raw and cooked food products to ensure that standards are met.
- Monitor sanitation practices to ensure that employees follow standards and regulations.
- Check the quantity and quality of received products.
- Demonstrate new cooking techniques and equipment to staff.
- Determine how food should be presented, and create decorative food displays.

Dietary aide & salad & dessert cook   2011

- Directed the preparation, seasoning, and cooking of salads, soups, fish, meats, vegetables, desserts or other foods.
- Determine how food should be presented and create decorative food displays.

JEREMY A. GOLDEN
12345 9TH STREET, NW * WASHINGTON, DC 20001   (202) 456-7890 * EMAIL: JAGOLDEN@MYMAIL.COM

SKILLS AND CERTIFICATIONS AS CERTIFIED TRADESMAN

- Coursework in Welder Certification
- Trained in Sheet Metal Work
- Facilities Maintenance
- Operates industrial maintenance equipment

Traffic/Flagger Certification
CPR/First Aid Certification
OSHA Certification
Inventory Tracking Experience

EDUCATION & TRAINING
Welding Coursework, Washington, DC   **2014-2018**
Approximately 400 hours of vocational training   **Continued Education**
GSA Building Futures Project   **2015**
Pre-apprenticeship training program with safety certifications and certificates of completion:
Blueprint reading, Orientation to Construction Industry, Introduction to Tools and Materials.

WORK HISTORY

NSC/Apprentice/Construction Contracting, Washington, DC   **Contract 2015**
- DC Government construction modernization projects at public schools
- Drywall, general laborer, painting and blueprint review and Foreman's top assistant
- Ensure safety procedures were maintained in accordance with state regulations.

HAZMAT/ Main Inspector, Washington, DC   **Contract 2015**
- Screens incoming mail for federal government departments preventing terrorism attacks of antrax and other chemical agents from carrying on mail to government facilities.
- Handle packing, loading and unloading mail to deliver.

Staples Office Movers, Washington, DC   **Contract 2010-2012**
- Carry on duties related to relocation responsibilities for government office moving from one location to the next.
- Conducted inventory of all furnishings to be transported, documented, and packaged to prevent damages and handled properly.

Facility Maintenance, Birmingham, AL   **2005 - 2009**
- Established and maintained stock reports of raw materials and finished goods.
- Conducted quality control inspections prior to and upon arrival of shipments.
- Operated and generated commercial bills of lading using SAP software system and Microsoft Excel
- Operated industrial maintenance equipment; proper use of industrial materials and chemicals.

Recreational Supervisor, Birmingham, AL   **2001-2002**
- Ensured releasing equipment was logged and accounted for; maintained workout equipment and supplies. Provided staff training, maintained schedules, and handled personnel matters.

This design allows the person to list their jobs during or after their release as contract positions.

ALLEN G. DAWKINS
111 Saint Paul's Avenue
Washington, DC 20000
202-123-9876
agdawkins@yahoo.com

Objective: to find a quality of customer service job. I am a dedicated, team player with attention to detail and leadership skills.

Owings Mill Cardiology

Records Processor   12/14 – 2/2018

Answered phones and handled records. Employed problem-solving techniques with patients and employees. Filed records and made copies. Performed routine duties as required.

George Washington library

Library assistant   3/10 – 12/2012

Assisted customers with library computer systems. Issued library cards and other library materials. Retrieved and processed daily circulation reports. Collected fines for non-return of books. Offered all services per request of library customers.

Education:
TC Williams High School – Completed 11th grade
References available upon request

ALLEN G. DAWKINS

111 Saint Paul's Ave* Washington, DC 20000, 202-123-9876, agdawkins@yahoo.com

---

CUSTOMER SERVICE SKILLS

Understands customer satisfaction	Strong communication and people skills
Flexible in schedule	Willing to listen and learn
Microsoft computer skills	Self- motivated and self-directed

Records Processor   12/14 – 2/2019
OWINGS MILL CARDIOLOGY

- Provided public relations support in a number of capacities.
- Employed problem-solving techniques with patients and employees.
- Ensured patient lab reports and corresponding charts and other documentation were accurate and available to hospital staff upon request.
- Performed routine duties such as purchasing office supplies and other needs as required.

Library Assistant   3/10 – 12/2012
GEORGE WASHINGTON LIBRARY

- Assisted customers with library computer systems.
- Issued library cards and other library materials.
- Retrieved and processed daily circulation reports.
- Collected fines for non-return of books.
- Offered all services per request of library customers.

(NOTE: If the individual has performed duties while incarcerated, it should be documented as job experience.)

Equipment Assembler
DEPARTMENT OF CORRECTIONS   1/92-7/2009

- Responsible for the assessment, repair, and installation of air vent equipment.
- Created assessment logs for determining when repairs would be completed.
- Documented and performed daily inventory on equipment and tools.
- Trained and supervised entry-level assemblers.

EDUCATION: Currently enrolled in work-study program. Expected graduation 7-2019

Why Do People Still Use Applications?

That's a good question. Everything requires some type of data collection related to finding employment. Since everybody's résumé will be formatted differently, it's more time-consuming to do the evaluation. An application helps to standardize the information companies collect and scan without using the standard application assessment. Do you remember when people had to go in to the company to fill out applications? And yet, even in our technological age, a large portion of companies still use applications.

When filling out an online application, be sure to answer all of the questions. If they are questions that do not relate to you, it's better to answer 'not applicable' than not answer it at all primarily because it looks suspicious. You can't apply for the job if you can't follow instructions. Your objective needs to be short, simple, and direct. Just list the job title itself. One mistake people often make is offering either too much detail (a novel) or not enough.

Example: Customer Service Representative/Support

Software programs are designed to focus on "key words." So what does that mean? Because online applications go directly into a database, and résumés are first scanned, every time the phrase "customer service" is posted, it brings your application forward, giving it a chance of being seen or read. Utilize the key words used in the advertisement to make the connection between your experience and the position requirements.

As an example, the next time you pick up a magazine, notice that certain words in the headline pull your attention to read it. Considering there are hundreds of pages and articles, certain words in the article will draw your attention to the content.

I also suggest mailing a hard copy of your résumé even though you've e-mailed it. Sometimes companies specifically say not to do so. If the option is available, use it. Always keep a backup copy on a thumb drive as well as a hard copy so you can easily make changes. (Just because you save it online doesn't mean it will be there forever.)

I realize that some of the suggestions I have made throughout the book seem to be common sense, right? I think you'd be surprised to know how much common sense people don't have when it comes to applying for employment. If you already know it, consider this a mini-review of information that may have been forgotten.

Proofreading—A Critical Elimint (*this is deliberate*)

Employers have made me painfully aware that proofreading is a critical element. They might be willing to overlook one typographical error, but two may blow your chance for an actual interview. That's why proofreading is not to be taken lightly. Employers believe there is absolutely no way you can be an effective candidate when something is amiss with your résumé. Since your résumé is your first impression, it should be reviewed with precision. Some managers have told me they will throw away an application if they find one error, because it indicates the job candidate is not thorough. Give your résumé to someone else to proofread. Someone else can provide a more objective perspective.

Since spell check certainly doesn't catch every mistake, you should put in the extra time required to ensure your information is complete. Make sure you don't throw away an opportunity by handing in sloppy work. I got this gem from resumania.com.

Case in point. . . . .

"I am sure you have looked through several resumes with the same information about work experience, education, and referrences. I am not going to give you any of that stuff."

"Please don't regard my 14 positions as job-hopping. I never once quit a job." "They stooped paying me."

"I am attacking my resume for you to review."

"I realize that my total lack of appropriate experience may concern those considering me, needles to say, I am willing to work hard to proof myself."

"Thank you for your consideration. Hope to hear from you shorty."

I rest my case!

Texting and Résumés Don't Mix

Considering this is the generation of text-speak, most people have a familiarity with this writing style. However, CUL8R, LOL, DND, GSA, and BTW mean absolutely nothing to a recruiter other than that you are too lazy to write complete sentences. This is a big no-no! O, BTW, this rule even gos when writg emal to other foks within ur cmpny. U no.

Résumé Designs That Don't Work!

Have you ever seen a résumé that made you want to say, "Oh no, he didn't!" Recruiters certainly have. That's why I am including this list of recruiters' biggest pet peeves. Some of these things are just annoying, and some are deal breakers. These suggestions are from the website: www.Resumedoctor.com. This website offers free templates, free designs, and free résumé evaluation. What a great place to start.

Top Recruiter Pet Peeves about Résumés

Use this list of errors to avoid to review your résumé.

♦ spelling errors, typos, and poor grammar
♦ meaningless objectives or introductions
♦ poor font choice or style
♦ missing dates or inaccurate dates
♦ too many gaps in employment
♦ unprofessional e-mail addresses
♦ using text-speak within your résumé
♦ poor formatting
♦ long, dense paragraphs in the résumé
♦ unqualified candidates applying to positions but lacking basic requirements
♦ personal information not relevant to the job
♦ missing employer information and/or not telling what industry or product candidate worked in
♦ lying or misleading, especially in terms of education, dates, and inflated titles
♦ too duty-oriented—reads like a job description that shows no accomplishments
♦ pictures, graphics, or URL links that no recruiter will call up

PART 4

References and Recommendations

References and Recommendations

Normally, the final entry listed at the bottom of most résumés is "References available upon request." Let's presume that all employers will require references. Just to make the hiring process simple, list your references on your résumé or attach them with your application. This way, the information is readily available if the employer wants it. Typically, if people are reading your résumés, they will likely read your references because it is attached. Much like when you read a letter, your natural inclination is to read all that is with it. It's also best to list at least two to three professional references and one personal reference. Sounds easy, right?

I *know* I need a reference, but . . .

What if the company I worked for nine years ago no longer exists?

This is where you've got to go through the back door to get the same result. You don't need a reference from your every company you've worked for, just list the company, the city, state and its' specialty: carpentry, furniture sales, etc. There are some well-known companies that are no longer in business. Simply use the phrases like 'department shutdown, relocation or no longer in business, rather than 'no longer exists'.

What if I got fired from the job?

You can list the company, but not a reference from that job. Never put a colleague in a position to lie on your behalf. First, it kills your relationship with them; and then places doubts in their mind about your character in other areas (of your life).

"What if I don't/didn't get along with my supervisor?" You're not required to list your direct supervisor. A reference is someone who can attest to your character and why you would be successful in the position. Just ensure that they can be reached by phone!

What if you don't have anybody from a previous company to list?

There are a number of other sources you can use as well. As an example a pastor, a mentor, a sponsor or even a parole officer. Yes, I said a parole officer. They may be the only current connections you have. They have the title that commands respect. They can attest to their experience in working with you in rebuilding your life. If you have been consistent in your relationship with them, yes, they can be utilized as a reference. However, you are *not* required to describe your relationship as parole officer, but use the term 'supervisor' in the capacity of relationship.

Let's discuss another reference people are not always aware is utilized today: Your Credit Report! How is that relevant to a job? Well, I'm glad you asked. Companies use your credit score as an indicator of the type of person you are based on how you pay your bills. While it may not be fair, it is a standard in today's employment requirements. Companies also look you up on Facebook, LinkedIn, Twitter and any other online medium to assess your character, your personality, even your friendships.

Case in point: on one of the segments on the *Dr. Phil show* was the subject about the economy and why it's so difficult to find a job. Now, the guest seemed to be an articulate, charming, intelligent and attractive young lady. Her résumé seemed to be in tact. Her credit rating was not the best, but wouldn't be an obstacle. BUT. . . they searched for her online and found a photo of her. I'm paraphrasing here, but something like . . . . time to kick back for the weekend. The picture looked like she had just done a line of cocaine. The HR guest said, clearly, that would be a deal-breaker! My first reaction was, so what? It's the weekend, right? There should be no harm in enjoying fun with friends. How will the fact that you had a party with your friends have impact on your ability to get your job done? Well, if you were to come in with a hangover, there's no doubt it will have an impact your work productivity that is *if* you come in at all. Now, I'm not saying you can't post pictures online on your own time, just be aware that once it is online, it can be used off-line – get it?

Next up: Always get permission from your references to list them beforehand so when they are contacted, they won't answer 'Who's that?' Information you should have for your references include job title, an active phone number and e-mail addresses of at least four people willing to serve as references. Let's be honest, I know it's not easy to stay connected with people who have known you throughout your entire career, but reaching out to people is the only way to get what you need. Of course technology certainly makes it easier. But don't let a reference stand in the way of a potential opportunity.

Other solid references would include:

♦ college fraternity networks
♦ personal counselors
♦ pastor/minister
♦ volunteer or charity organizer
♦ professors/faculty members
♦ next door neighbor

Below are three different examples of recommendation styles which might be helpful in designing yours. Of course, no one size fits all here. Each of these are samples is designed specifically for people with inconsistent work histories.

Sample I

To the Director of Personnel:

I am truly excited to hear about Katherine's opportunity to work with your Pet and People Project. I am also grateful that you see her as a candidate for future growth within your company. She recognizes that nothing will be handed to her, but a firm believer that she must work to prove herself and her abilities. I am sure you will recognize her work style and personality will make a great contribution for your program. The fact that Katherine previously worked with Petco means she can easily relate to having love and compassion for your four-legged family.

Natalie's history does not define the person that she is today or diminished her spirit to move forward in a positive manner. I hope you find this to be true and that she can be given a chance to work toward a more successful future for herself and her daughter.

If you have any need to contact me directly, please do not hesitate to do so. Once again, I am extremely proud of Katherine and more importantly her desire to succeed.

Respectfully,

Natalie Andrews

Sample II

RECOMMENDATION FOR KEVIN E. YARD

I am pleased to be able to recommend Kevin Yard for a full-time help desk position. While I have only worked with Kevin for one year, it doesn't surprise me that his efforts have been noticed within other departments.

His enthusiastic take charge personality
As I have been his supervisor, I can attest that his level of enthusiasm is contagious within our department. Kevin has a way of making everyone who works around him a part of the team. He has been called upon to conduct employee training and assist others in the absence of one of the immediate supervisors. He has leadership qualities that come through in his communication style and make him a pleasure to work with. I've personally observed his co-workers respect his judgment in handling various customer situations. This makes my job easier when there is a second 'go-to guy who can make sound decisions.

His excellent customer service skills
Kevin is a personable individual whose skills and knowledge are exceptional. On several occasions I have spoken to clients he has supported and received compliments for his level of patience, clarity and confidence. Kevin takes pride in his commitment to not just give out scripted information, but to go above and beyond to achieve customer satisfaction. On the average, we receive two or three comments per week which reflects this.

Our loss, your gain
You've probably gathered that we would have a difficult time replacing someone of Mr. Yard's personality, skill and attitude. However, we aren't disappointed that he'll be moving on to more successful opportunities. Our loss would favorably be your gain. We wish the best for Kevin in his next endeavors.

Sincerely,

Mr. Gregory Grass
Information Services Director

Sample III

This sample of multiple recommendations comes from a different perspective instead of one more formal letter. This can be used with someone with either a sporadic work history, volunteer work history or a less than a stellar one.

REFERENCES FROM MANAGEMENT AND COLLEAGUES
4/2016 - 5/2019

Working with Kevin has been a pleasure. He has given me a better perspective on building relationships with customers to ensure they keep coming back. He has consistently been praised for his response time in handling a number of situations. Way to go, Kevin.
Edna Milton, Accountant

Kevin's energy seems to light up the room when he's here in the office. It's obvious you can see that he loves what he does and shows it every day.
Margaret Walsh, Postal Driver

Kevin is always willing to take on more responsibilities with a smile. When working with the clients over the phone he is always patient and willing offers the best recommendations.
Martin Shelly, Customer Service Rep.

The education that Mr. Yard lacks leaves more of his talent. His communication skills, his adaptability, his attitude and his willingness to learn supersedes his experience.
Tony Carson, Regional Director

If I were working for your company I would hire Kevin in a minute!

Luis Estrada, Consultant

Since I have been the director of the Meals on Wheels (MOW) program, Kevin has always had a driven passion to help others and we are proud that he was willing to volunteer his time with us. Many of the recipients are homebound and need support. Kevin not only helped in delivery, but he managed the weekly delivery of 150 meals to our residents 60 years or older. I can't say enough about Kevin and it is our hope that he receives this opportunity he so richly deserves.

Tina Watson, Program Manager

(When using this format the use of snippets have a much higher impact from multiple sources since it shows a diversity of work environments.)

Dealing with Discouragement and Disappointment: When the Job Doesn't Come Fast Enough

Job-hunting can be a grueling and emotional experience. You will face plenty of rejection and will hit brick walls from time to time. You can spend weeks following a hot lead only to find that the job has already been filled. So, how are you supposed to handle this and still have a positive attitude?

Before fighters go into the ring, they are already prepared to take some solid blows. Before going in, they make use of a few key techniques in order to focus on the goal rather than the pain. That's why determination is most important. It's not just about a positive attitude. It's about determination! Here's a typical scenario. You see a job posted online. You think it looks like a great fit for your skills and interests. You attach your résumé or online application and anxiously await a response. You wait…and wait…and wait. No one calls—there is no response.

Anticipate waiting a minimum of four weeks before receiving a response and you'll feel less anxiety while you wait. When you don't get an immediate response, consider these factors before giving up:

a) you weren't the best candidate for the job.
b) your résumé may have been misplaced
c) it may be sitting in someone's e-mail with fifty others
d) the position has already been filled
e) they decided not to fill the position to save money

In the meantime, take the initiative to follow up. Even go through the effort of sending another résumé or thank you note in advance. Here are seven steps to take when the search takes more out of you than you've got.

Remember, the person who is hungriest is the one who will get fed!

♦ Determine *why* you want this job in advance. What is it that will keep you focused in the face of discouragement?

> (*Example:* I want to ensure my family has security. I want peace of mind, retirement, etc.)

♦ Study your opponent. Look at employment statistics and other information.

> (*Example:* This field is growing, and I have experience. I can go back to school to obtain the necessary degree.)

♦ Be extremely conscious of the people you spend time with during what could be a difficult time. Be sure to spend time with people who lift you up, keep you smiling, and can offer you insight and direction.

> (*Example:* The people you want around you are people who want the best for you.)

♦ Keep yourself emotionally, physically and spiritually fit. Fighters work out 8–10 hours a day for months before a fight.

♦ This is where fit, faith, and function come together. Exercise and spend time quality time in meditation and prayer.

♦ Know what to do when you get hit with a good punch.

> (*Example:* Don't react out of panic. Be prepared to take a step back and take inventory of what you should have done. Reevaluate, recharge, and reset. Consider it a learning and a lesson.)

♦ Join a network of people in the same general age group who are also looking for jobs. People bond when they share similar experiences. Within a networking group, you can celebrate with others as they achieve the goals, and it offers others hope. As you find leads, you can forward them to others. In other words, pay it forward—even when you haven't gotten paid.

Anticipate setbacks, but don't let them set you back! Persist until you succeed. In today's economy, it can take people from six months to a year or more to find a job! Determination is achievement in spite of the pain. Understand that it won't be an easy journey.

"It's supposed to be hard. If it wasn't hard everyone would do it. The hard is what makes it great."
Tom Hanks, *A League of Their Own*

PROFESSIONAL ACTION PLAN
Now that you know, how will you grow?

I have designed this page to give you the opportunity to determine what valuable information you have received and how you can implement strategies discussed in each chapter.

1. _____

2. _____

3. _____

4. _____

5. _____

6. _____

Putting A Price On Your Appearance

CHAPTER 12

PROJECT RUNWAY FOR YOUR INTERVIEW

While you are waiting for your résumé to generate some job interviews, you should assess your appearance and wardrobe and make sure you have what it takes to present the *professional* you! For people who say, "I don't have a lot of money," I'd suggest you don't need a lot of money to display style. Start with some of the pieces in your closet and set a budget of $50 per piece. (of course, check your bank account first)

Your style first and foremost needs to be a reflection of who you are, with a combination of dress-up as well as dress-down styles that fit your personality and culture. In order to determine your style, I would first go to a clothing store—like Macy's (my favorite place)—with a friend and pick out five different outfits. A friend can be a little more objective, because he or she is somewhat familiar with your wardrobe. Let your friend help you put together a combination of pieces. Many HR managers have told me they decided against hiring an applicant based on they dressed. So, when *was* the last time you did a wardrobe check? What year – 200?? Can't even remember, huh?

What does your clothing say about you? The official term is "style." Do you have a comfortable, but classic style like Michelle Obama's or are you a trend-setter like Lady Gaga? For men, would you say you have more in common with George Clooney or Elton John? I'll use myself as a prime example. When I transitioned from the military I didn't know what style was, let alone that I needed to have one. How do you establish your own personal signature style without standing out in a negative way? First, you need to evaluate your wardrobe. Go through every piece from your shoes, your purse and even your jewelry. For men, it's shoes, ties, shirts, jackets and watches.

To assess your clothes, look at how many sizes you have in your closet. The size you used to wear, the size you currently wear, and the sizes you've worn along the way. A woman's body type often changes as she ages. It's a little different for men. Oh, calm down! I'm not saying men don't change as well, but men r-a-r-e-l-y get pregnant, so . . . . you see my point. They generally maintain one size and one style throughout their lives. My brothers still have some of the same sweatshirts, T-shirts, and jeans they wore in college. I've always wondered—*what is that about?* Since people don't usually get rid of the clothes they don't wear, our closets become treasure chests of *bad* fashion!

For men, I'd recommend having someone at your side to give some guidance. No, I'm not being sexist. My husband is color-blind, so a majority of his clothes were either brown, black or dark blue. It's just a suggestion, okay? One of the reasons I didn't like shopping is because I didn't understand my own dress style so I didn't know what I was buying or why.

In addition to interview outfits, you should also have the following accessories: watches, earrings, stockings, and even underclothing. You don't have to have a three-piece suit, but you definitely need a complete combination for any occasion.

For men, a dress shirt, tie, dress slacks, and jacket will suffice. Oh, yeah, a jacket isn't always a necessity, but again, the position you're applying for will determine the style of dress. Keep in mind that you may not be in the corporate environment, so always consider what kind of social clothing you have for when you're just out in a casual setting, networking with clients or enjoying time on a Friday with your colleagues. Let me say this before I get attacked: if you work in a tattoo shop, obviously, a suit is not required. If your job is to drop off parts for a mechanic shop, again, you're in good shape. However, you need to consider the type of industry you would be working in before and after you find the job.

For women comfortable conservative is the way to go. Stock up on outfits that demonstrate an understanding of the work environment. Keep things casual and professional. Try to use sharp colors. I also like to use the term "smooth combos." An example would be to look at the store mannequins combos just to get a feel of the fashion. It doesn't mean that you can't add a little pop in your wardrobe. Don't forget the clothing that usually goes "under the radar," so to speak: stockings and underclothing, purses, and makeup.

What Not to Wear
- If you can wear it to the club, don't wear it to work.
- If people will spend more time determining your bra size than listening to your conversation, don't wear it to work.
- If it clings more than it sings, don't wear it to work.
- If you can wear it to a picnic, don't wear it to work.
- If you can wear it to a football game, don't wear it to work.

Whether you're interviewing for the job or you get the job, you represent yourself *first!* Then you represent your department, organization or the company that hires you. One technique I used was to evaluate the style of local and national news anchors because they usually show the trend of professional environment in today. Think the *Today Show* or *Good Morning America*. This advice is for men as well as women.

Now, don't underestimate the importance of taking a shower, shaving, neatly styling your hair, and brushing your teeth before going to an interview as well.

People would rather interview someone who is clean and boring than dirty and stylish.

While I'm sure some of the material we've just covered you've heard before, but a lot of the professional wardrobe rules have changed over the years. So, for those of you who have extensive experience in the workplace, this may enlighten you on the newest acceptable fashion trends in the workplace today. If you've been in the workplace within the past seven to ten years, you are pretty hip on what employers expect and will accept regarding wardrobe. Some of the material presented will refresh your understanding of the current acceptable trends in the workplace, and if you've just begun your journey into the professional world, this chapter will prep you for the expectations of the office wardrobe or what they expect you to know, but won't always say to you, but will say to someone else.

Just like technology has expanded our office environments, diversity in culture also expands our diversity of dress for people of various religious beliefs. This means that they will hold firmly to their faith even in their dress style. I believe, if it doesn't cross the line, then it's fine. At some point, if it were to cause any type of concern, the human resource's role is to make corrections if it's necessary. It's not your job to be the 'fashion police'.

The Benefits of Online Clothes Shopping
Since more and more people like the option of online shopping, below are a few websites you may want to take a look at.

www.macys.com
Can we all agree that most people are on some kind of budget? The reason I add Macy's to my list is that Macy's has a reputation for high-end clothing, but you can find deals there that work with your budget and still give you the confidence that you're wearing clothes that say style. I strongly suggest you add them as "favorites" in your browser.

www.menswarehouse.com
So, what makes this a gem? Looking for women's wear is a snap. But looking for men's wear is truly a challenge if you have a tight budget. Okay, keep in mind

that high-end men's wear is *not* cheap—$299 and up. However, if you're looking for quality, I'd start here.

www.kgstores.com

Fashion for less! They have sales like you wouldn't believe. Buy one suit; get three free! I'm talking "Big and Tall" and full-size collections for men and women. This is a store that offers true combinations for the interview closet, including ties, jackets, socks, and watches. Yes, I know I sound like an advertisement, but that's how good it is!

www.MyShape.com

This site allows users to create a store of their own, in which nothing but items that fit their *exact measurements* are listed, from dresses to pajamas. Once you submit your measurements, you'll be presented with clothes and garments that are sure to look flawless on you.

www.Pinterest.com/Marywoodcareer

This is a great site and lots of fun. First, Marywood Career site caters to the college job-hunting crowd, from student interns to alumni, as well as those interested in casual campus wear. This website does a wonderful job of incorporating a number of key ingredients in developing a wardrobe including "fun-wear." It has a nice blend of wardrobes displayed in magazines as well as designs that you can assess to determine your own clothing needs.

Most professional environments have "business casual" dress codes. That means you should leave the halter tops, flip-flops, Bermuda shorts, cleavage display, tattoos and belly piercings for nights out with your friends. It doesn't matter how down-to-earth or casual your boss is, they still needs to see you as a professional.

Below is an Internet funny that sums up this section quite nicely. Enjoy!

Corporate Policies and Procedures:

1. You are advised to come to work dressed according to your salary.
2. If we see you wearing Prada shoes and carrying a bag by Lady Gaga, we will assume you are doing well financially and therefore do not need a raise.
3. If you dress poorly, you need to learn to budget your money better so that you may buy nicer clothes, and therefore you do not need a raise.
4. If you dress just right for your salary, you are right where you need to be, and therefore you do not need a raise.
5. SICK DAYS: We will no longer accept a doctor's statement as proof of sickness. As long as the respirator is working, there should be no problems with working at your desk.
6. PERSONAL DAYS: Each employee will receive 104 personal days a year. They are called Saturdays and Sundays.
7. BATHROOM BREAKS: Entirely too much time is being spent in the toilet. There is now a strict three-minute time limit in the stalls. At the end of three minutes, an alarm will sound, the toilet paper roll will retract, the stall door will open, and a picture will be taken. After your second offense, your picture will be posted on the company Facebook page under the "Chronic Offenders" category. Anyone caught smiling in the picture will be sanctioned under the company's mental health policy.
8. LUNCH BREAK: Underweight people get twenty minutes for lunch, as they need to eat more, so they can look healthy.
   Average size people get fifteen minutes for lunch to get a balanced meal to maintain their clothing size.

If you work anywhere in customer service, don't bother to sit down for lunch, just drink a *"Red Bull"* and keep going.

Thank you in advance for your loyalty to our company. We are here to provide a positive employment experience. Therefore, all questions, concerns, comments, complaints, frustrations, irritations, aggravations, insinuations, allegations, accusations, contemplations, consternations, and input should be directed wherever you find your next job.

The Management
www.thatwasfunny.com/policies-and-procedures
(Come on—that was funny!)

PART 6

Why People Hate Interviewing

Understanding the Interviewing Process

O ne of the biggest obstacles to finding a job is the dreaded 'Interview!" People have a variety of reasons for hating interviews, but overall the underlying reason is often fear. Some of the most challenging clients to interview is someone with a criminal background transitioning to a new job or being out of the workplace for some time. Knowing the question is coming, but not confident in how to respond causes anxiety. While there are issues with interviewing that have nothing to do with having the perfect answer, like being shy, understanding the interviewing process can help to reduce those fears.

So, where does fear come from? Fear begins in the mind and then compounds itself as we make comparisons of ourselves to others. Fear also grows from the belief that we will be rejected in the interviewing process. As you review this list, see if you can identify any fears you may have experienced.

Fear!

♦ People are unsure of how to handle certain questions.
♦ People are shy or nervous when meeting strangers.
♦ People are afraid of saying the wrong thing.
♦ People anticipate the trick question.
♦ People are unsure of how to explain major gaps in employment.
♦ People lack confidence in their abilities.
♦ People are afraid of freezing up.
♦ People are often embarrassed by their own perceived lack of experience.
♦ People often have negative thinking patterns that make interviews stressful.
♦ People overanalyze the questions.

◆ People try to come up with the perfect answer instead of simply answering the question.

◆ People are afraid of exposing weaknesses.

◆ People don't know how to cope with the stigma attached to previous incarcerations, mental health issues, addictions, or previous terminations.

CHAPTER 13

TOP TEN SECRETS TO DIFFERENT INTERVIEWING STYLES

First, and most is to determine the needs of the employer before walking in the door. Second in preparing for a job interview, familiarize yourself with interviewing styles you may encounter. That way you won't be caught off guard if you walk into a room to be interviewed and there are more people there than you expect, or if the interviewer doesn't just ask the most common types of questions.

The Power of Your Handshake

It's the day of your interview, and you're about to meet someone for the first time. A handshake is not something you do to be cordial; it's expected! Whether you are a professional, an intern, or meeting someone at a casual event, something as simple as a handshake can leave a powerful impression. A handshake says confidence, credibility, and character all at the same time. Have you ever shaken someone's hand and thought to yourself *really?*

Yes, there is a correct way to shake hands. Let me explain. A handshake communicates on three levels. There needs to be a sense of firm confidence that says, "I know who I am." It says, "I know why I'm here." And more importantly, it says, "I'm the one for the job." Is it the same for women? You bet. There should be no differentiation between the sexes on this one.

A solid handshake acknowledges the other person and demonstrates your sense of confidence. In one of my blogs, I wrote about what attracts employers to a potential job candidate. Yes, a candidate's handshake made the list. Why? Because it's the employer's first personal interaction with the job candidate. He or she has read your credentials; now he or she wants to meet the person behind them.

The protocol is this: When someone introduces you, you always stand, smile, make eye contact, and repeat the person's name. This will ensure that you can remember it later. It leaves a wonderful impression, because it says you understand protocol. While our culture says a head nod is a reasonable acknowledgment, a handshake is the professional one. I recommend an article by Kevin Eikenberry in the May 2011 *Toastmasters* magazine entitled "How to Make a Good First Impression." It focuses specifically on the protocol of meeting someone for the first time.

As a rule, when you offer your hand first, it shows receptivity and warmth. Keep your hand open and make sure your handshake will be a *hand* shake and not a wrist, finger, palm shake or fist bump. Make your grip firm, and adjust it to the firmness of the other person's grip. Learn to give a great handshake. Practice it, and make it your habit when meeting anyone—whether it's an instructor, a visitor, or a guest.

With that said, let's look at things you can do that immediately turn people off!

- ◆ *Not standing up to greet others.* That is a true sign of disrespect; it indicates laziness.
- ◆ *Lack of eye contact.* I'm sure you'll agree that you expect people to look you in the eye when they speak to you. It's even more critical if you're speaking with the interviewer. When you don't, it sends the signal that the interviewer isn't important enough to command your attention.
- ◆ *The limp wrist.* This communicates a lack of authority. You should demonstrate authority in your handshake, your walk, and your talk.

♦ *Squeezing too tightly.* This suggests you are trying to impress with physical strength.

♦ *Shaking hands with your fingers.* This is not an actual handshake and signals discomfort with touching someone.

♦ *Not smiling.* A smile is a part of your handshake; not smiling suggests that you are not personable or easy to get along with.

Think of your handshake as a résumé. Show your positive attributes up front so that employers will remember you later.

Traditional Face-to-Face Interview

Most of the time, interviews are face-to-face, which involves one-on-one conversation. Please make sure that you focus on the person asking the questions. Your goal is to establish rapport and build commonality with the interviewer. Show the interviewer how your qualifications will benefit the organization or department and your personality with the team.

Panel/Committee Interview

There is more than one interviewer in this type of situation. Several members of the panel may conduct this part of the selection process. Please adjust to each interviewer as needed so that you can connect with each panelist as an individual. Maintain primary eye contact with the panel member who asked you the question, but also seek eye contact with other members of the panel as you respond. Also ensure you use the name of the person who asked the question.

These questions typically start with "Give me an example when…" or, "Tell about a time when…"

Stress Interview

This type of interview is a deliberate attempt to see how you handle yourself under pressure. The interviewer may be argumentative or combative. Perhaps the interviewer might keep you waiting. Calmly answer all questions and ask the interviewer to repeat the questions if necessary. The interviewer may lapse into silence during the interview. Sit quietly until the interviewer résumés questioning. In this style of interview, focus on the questions and not your emotional response to the interviewer.

Informational Interview

On the opposite end of the stress spectrum is the informational interview. It is less formal, and the job seeker is seeking advice from someone who works in their desired field. The purpose of the interview is to gain additional insight about a given position without the pressure of an official interview.

Behavioral Interview

In this type of interview, the interviewer will often offer a scenarios to determine how he or she would respond in a given situation. These questions may be asked over the phone, in a one-on-one setting, or in a panel. The responses need to be answered based on facts, and the interview is looking for results. More specifically, the interviewer is looking for the role you played in the results, while listening for names, dates, places, specific actions you took, and the outcome.

Skype Teleconference Interview

Because technology is so expansive, many companies now conduct interviews via webcam and using applications such as Skype. This allows companies to interview candidates who are geographically distant. This reduces travel costs and other expenses. The candidate will need to access a web camera, but the interview can be conducted anywhere. When you have this type of interview, it is critical to limit the distractions as much as possible—kids, pets, phones, and other distractions. Have a copy of your résumé handy. Remember not to relax your standards; your interviewers won't.

The Audition Interview

This interview works best for positions requiring visual skills, such as actors, professional speakers or trainers, equipment repair, or athletes. Employers want to see candidates in action before they make their decision. An audition can be enormously useful to you, since it allows you to demonstrate your skills in person for more impact. Just remember to listen carefully to the interviewer's request to ensure you respond completely.

The Group Interview

This is usually designed to uncover the leadership potential of prospective managers and employees who will be working with customers. The front-runner candidates are gathered in a discussion-type interview. The interviewer introduces a topic and begins the discussion. The goal of this type of interview is to see how well you interact with others and how well you use your knowledge and reasoning to influence others.

Lunch/Dinner Interview

Interviewing at lunch or dinner gives the experience of a much more relaxed environment. Don't let the environment fool you, though; it's still an interview. Depending on the position you're interviewing for, you may be required to interact with clients or other personnel. Follow the interviewer's lead and establish commonalities in conversation and atmosphere. Don't overindulge just because someone else is paying the tab; don't order an alcoholic drink even if one is offered.

Final and Follow-up Interview

If your first interviews have been successful, the follow-up interview can help to solidify the relationship to move further. If you weren't in the running, they wouldn't be calling you back. But don't celebrate yet. The job may be down to you and one other candidate, and this final interview will determine who gets the prize. If you have not heard anything after the third or fourth day after the interview, take the initiative to follow up with an e-mail and then contact the person by phone. Remember, you want to keep that lasting impression by speaking with him or her and build a strong connection.

For More Information about Interview Styles

For more information about types of interviews, I recommend you go to www.interviewsuccessformula.com. This website is a gem. It uses a number of techniques to help you identify and understand the purpose of each style of interviewing.

PART 7

The Question Behind The Interview Question

CHAPTER 14

WHAT DOES THAT MEAN?

So, what's this chapter about? Well, when someone is asking a question, in many cases there is an answer that people would like to hear on the other end. Case in point: The question is, what are you doing?' usually means 'I know you're getting into something.' Usually it's the answer that will best benefit their goal. The reason this chapter is so critical is that it prepares you to put the employer's fear at ease. This segment allows you to peek into the mind of someone who asks questions with specific answers in mind. As I said before, there's no such thing as the perfect answer, but there are effective answers.

You'll notice that television advertisements basically sum up the "why I should buy" factor before they ask for the sale. That's your goal. Don't let those jitters get in the way of the product. Today we will put you in the employer's seat. (Comfy, huh?) Before we discuss what your answers to specific questions should be, let's look at how you can create the best first impression, before you even open your mouth.

> *Remember: market your product -- you!*

Common Interview Questions and What They Really Mean

Okay, based on my own personal interviews with a number of headhunters, HR directors, job placement counselors, and coaches, these are the questions that often go through the mind of the interviewer. Let's look at what the employer is really trying to discover by asking these questions.

When the interviewer asks:

"How did you find out about the position?"

HIDDEN QUESTION:

Which method works best in finding good candidates – online, referral or other.

When the interviewer asks:

"Why did you want to apply for his job?" or "Why do you want to be a ____?"

HIDDEN QUESTION:

Are you looking for something short-term or longevity, growth and opportunities?

When the interviewer asks:

"What would you consider to be your biggest strengths?"

HIDDEN QUESTION:

"Will the qualities you offer be a benefit to our company?"

Potential answer could be: I've always believed my greatest strengths are my management skills and my ability to handle pressure with humor. Of course, I have lots of other strengths, but I won't tell you until I get the job.

*(This is your opportunity to sell, sell, and sell yourself! Do **not** use phrases like "dependable," "hardworking," or "team player.")*

When the interviewer asks:

"What is your biggest weakness?"

HIDDEN QUESTION:

Can you identify your shortcomings and compensate for them?

Potential answer could be: "I'll be honest. I've always struggled with proofreading. It's a skill I've never mastered. But I've learned to slow down and to focus on the task rather than to rush the process."

Everybody has at least one weakness, so don't ever say you don't have any. Employers have told me they look down on an answer like that because it proves the person is not genuine.

When the interviewer asks:
"What are your goals over the next five years?"

Potential answer could be: "I'm really looking to put down some permanent roots with a company and build my experience."

HIDDEN QUESTION:
Are you looking to develop your long-term goals with the company?

When the interviewer asks:
"Are you willing to work overtime periodically?"

HIDDEN QUESTION:
"Can we count on you to be available when it's necessary?"

Potential answer could be: "I am still going to school, but I'm sure I can work around my schedule when it's needed." Okay, here's the part of the book where you put your skills to work with the information I just gave you. Your assignment is to prepare *your own personal answers* to the questions below based on your own experience. Go ahead; you can do it!

When the interviewer asks:
"Why did you leave your last job?"

HIDDEN QUESTION:

_____

_____

Potential answer could be:

_____

_____

When the interviewer asks:
"What sort of starting salary are you looking for?"

HIDDEN QUESTION:

_____

_____

Potential answer could be:

_____

_____

When the interviewer asks:
"I see you're a single mom; will that affect your scheduling?"

HIDDEN QUESTION:

_____

_____

Potential answer could be:

_____

_____

Now, there are certain questions interviewers cannot ask because they are considered illegal. What I mean by illegal are questions related to age, disability, marital/family status, national origin, race, religion, or sexual orientation. However, it doesn't mean they won't ask these questions.

So, what should you do if one of these questions is asked? One of my favorite books is *Powerphrases*, written by a colleague of mine, Ms. Meryl Runion. Her book has a listing of office situations that offers insight into how to determine whether questions do indeed cross the professional line, and the best options for responding.

These are a number of potential responses:

- ◆ Yes, that is true; however, I'd prefer not to go into any detail…
- ◆ I'm not sure how to answer that question…
- ◆ I'm not sure I understand what you mean…

What Should You Say?

How should you respond to the question "Why did you leave your previous job?" It's an easy question if you had to relocate, you got another opportunity, or you were laid off. But what if you were fired or arrested or had to deal with alcoholism? What do you say or what is it you don't say?

Pastor John Hagee of Cornerstone Church of Houston, Texas, put it this one in one of his sermons: "Words have power, and power has effect."

His analogy was dead on. Negative words give off negative results because they suck you in to a negative mind-set. Our natural instinct is to envision the worst. Think about it. Certain words lead people to visualize what they think you mean. If you have ever asked someone for directions, the person giving the directions visualizes the road in his or her head. But the key here is you have to be able to visualize the directions in *your* head if you're going to get to the right place. That is the reason people still get lost even after getting directions. When you say "vacation," people tend to imagine beautiful beaches and expensive hotels. When you say "wedding," people envision handcuffs—just kidding—they might imagine a white dress or a large church. When you say "jail," you might imagine steel bars or an orange jumpsuit. Whatever the image might be, you get my point.

So, what do you imagine when you hear the word *fired?* The image in my head is probably not a good one. The image in our heads is usually the one we believe is true because we see it in our minds.

Rather than say "I was fired," explain, "I was let go because…" What associations do you have with the phrase "let go"? Did you visualize something different from what you visualized when you heard "fired"?

Let's look at a few words that might bring on the negative images:

♦ quit
♦ fired
♦ babysitting problems
♦ late/tardy
♦ not enough money
♦ couldn't get to work
♦ lawsuit
♦ arrested
♦ discrimination

When you hear the word *quit,* what comes to mind? My interpretation of the word *quit* is that someone walked off the job. But how do you interpret the word *resigned?* See my point? My challenge to you would be to take each word and come up with an alternative phrase that allows you to explain any of these scenarios without leaving a bad taste in your mouth. Okay, go ahead and try it. I already did three words; now it's your turn.

Quit	Resigned
Couldn't get to work	Transportation issues
Babysitting problems	Childcare availability
Fired	_____
Hours are too long	_____
Didn't make enough money	_____
Supervisor didn't like me	_____
Lawsuit	_____
Arrested	_____
Discrimination	_____
Manager didn't like me	_____

The Imprint of Words

Just as negative words leave a negative imprint so do 'power' words because they leave a much stronger visual imprint that add quality and value to the person. Keep in mind that as you create your résumés, you need to add a minimum of ten of these power words to *gain successful results*. See what I mean? Of course, these are just the tip of the iceberg. I expect you to complete the rest of the iceberg. 8-)

Here you go!

Achieve	Detail	Growth	Mission	Results	Target
Action	Effort	High	Opportunity	Return	Talent
Believe	Excellence	Increase	Prosper	Satisfy	Unique
Collect	Form	Integrity	Progress	Success	Value
Create	Focus	Improve	Produce	Support	Vision
Discover	Gather	Limitless	Receive	Specialize	

_____	_____	_____	_____	_____	_____
_____	_____	_____	_____	_____	_____
_____	_____	_____	_____	_____	_____
_____	_____	_____	_____	_____	_____

Your Professional Report Card

When I was growing up, I loved getting report cards! It was a wonderful experience, because I enjoyed getting written feedback on my progress. It helped me to know whether I was on track for the school year. (Plus, I always got good grades.) Okay, enough about me. Did you know that each time you interview you're being graded? Well, you are, but you'll never get the feedback in the interviewers' heads.

After sitting down with a number of HR managers and job placement directors, here's what they have told me regarding the secret interviewing grading system. I asked them, "What are you assessing when you're doing an interview?" And this is what they said they were evaluating:

♦ Does the candidate express him or herself well and present a solid professional image?
♦ What are the behavioral characteristics of this applicant?
♦ Does the applicant exhibit strong character?
♦ Will the applicant get along with members of the existing team?
♦ What are the applicant's strengths? What qualities does the applicant possess that others may lack?
♦ What type of initiative has this applicant shown during the application and interview process?
♦ Does the applicant possess leadership or supervisory skills?
♦ Did the applicant come prepared for the interview?
♦ What type of body language does the person display?
♦ Does the person display a positive or negative attitude concerning his or her past employer?
♦ Is the person an independent thinker?
♦ Do I see potential in that person?

Your interview is not just about your skills; it's also to determine whether your personality is the right fit in the structure of the office. People want to work with someone they can relate to naturally. The more relaxed the interview, the better your opportunity for hire.

Some interview questions are designed to get you to think on your feet. People often believe they have to the perfect answer. It's Okay to take a moment to think before you speak. If not, you'll be beating yourself up later.

If the interviewer asks if you have any questions, always ask some! Find out exactly what the company's expectations are for the position. Asking questions shows that you're relaxed—a trait employers value.

Just so you understand, your report card doesn't begin in the interview room; it begins in the lobby. I know of supervisors who deliberately make candidates wait to see how or if they interact with the front desk personnel. Then they will ask these staff members to give their assessment.

I was told if the candidate's cell phone goes off just once, he or she is out. It's a true sign of disrespect in the interviewers' eyes. They say Etiquette 101 is to turn off your electronic equipment. If you can't turn your phone off for an interview, it's a strong indicator you'll probably be on it throughout the workday.

> Every minute you're on your phone is money you take away from your employer!

While some of these suggestions may seem superficial, you'd be surprised at how much weight interviewers attach to these behaviors. Remember, this is your professional report card. Your job is to get a good grade.

How to Quit Your Job and Still Win!

What do you mean "quit a job?" It was hard enough to find one. I understand it's not a subject people like to talk about. But life happens. Quitting your job is not the worst thing that can happen. How you quit makes the difference.

Let's say your spouse gets transferred to another company, you've decided you'd rather go back to school full-time or be a stay-at-home parent, or you realize that your job is simply not working for you.

Just as finding a job is a process, so is quitting a job. You should employ the same level of professionalism you used to obtain the job when you leave it. You need to be prepared for the types of questions you will face when you tell your employer that you are leaving. You can never predict the reaction you're going to get—from anger to disappointment—so be prepared for the emotional side of the discussion as well. If you are an asset to the company, your employer will probably do everything possible to either talk you out of it or give a counter offer.

Does it matter why you quit your job?

You'd better believe it.

Be prepared to explain your reason for leaving. Do not offer too many details, though, or the discussion will turn into an interrogation. When you make that kind of decision, it can feel like rejection to the people at your job. It's not like telling everyone that you just purchased a home or you're getting married. People who have developed close relationships with you may not be prepared for your decision. Use as much tact as possible and determine the best time to let everyone know. Consider your decision as a celebration, and encourage everyone to celebrate with you.

Make sure it is in writing.

In order for your resignation to be official, you must submit it in writing. Offering a written, formal resignation is an opportunity to obtain closure. However, it is not an opportunity to document all of your grievances with the company. This is another case of K.I.S.S. (keep it short and sweet).

Consider your exit interview.

Some organizations require you to undergo an exit interview with HR (human resources) in order to meet specific guidelines. This is to explain the exit process regarding turning in corporate equipment, badges, corporate entitlements, insurance, health care, and nondisclosure agreements. This system protects the employer from disgruntled employees who might destroy documents. What most people do not know is that you are not *required* to do an exit interview.

If you are leaving under favorable circumstances, your supervisor may want to discuss whether you can suggest any areas of improvements that might be of benefit to the company. This is the one opportunity to voice your concerns without repercussions. But beware of how you express them. Use this is an opportunity to demonstrate your professionalism and class. If your comments can be of benefit to the organization, comment away. But if you're just using it as a tabloid attack, what you say could affect future recommendations. Often managers are hearing some of these things for the first time because no one else is bold enough to say them. However, if you feel the interview may leave debris behind, many people are not aware that you have the right to turn down an exit interview.

Finally, should you choose to have an exit interview, when discussing your reasons for leaving be honest, but more importantly be diplomatic.

PROFESSIONAL ACTION PLAN
Now that you know, how will you grow?

I have designed this page to give you the opportunity to determine what valuable information you have received and how you can implement strategies discussed in this chapter.

1. _____

2. _____

3. _____

4. _____

5. _____

6. _____

PART 8

The Art of Negotiation
Getting Paid What You're Worth

CHAPTER 16

SALARY SECRETS: HOW TO DETERMINE YOUR VALUE?

I'm sure that by now you've been counting your salary potential from the moment you started working on your résumé. Your salary potential depends on two key factors: your experience and your negotiation skills!

The definition of negotiation is "the ability to reach an agreement through discussion and compromise." A solid negotiation should be a conversation regarding your value to the company. Your competitors are applying for the same position. This is where your communication skills and your negotiation skills will set you apart. In this economy, you never want to overbid your talents, or you won't have the opportunity to show them off. But if you underbid, it can mean some time before you get paid what you are worth. Ask for what you want, and then compromise to get what you need.

It's also important to understand your industry, the job market, your specialty, your location, your years of experience, and, just as important, your longevity. Why longevity, you ask? If you are offered a good starting salary, it is the company's hope that you won't look for another job after your first year, because the pay is not right).

Consider whether the position is blue-collar, technical, administrative, or government. Many of these industries have structured pay scales. For example, military positions use rank to determine salary: private, lieutenant colonel, major, or captain. Government positions are listed as GS, which stands for general service.

If you are interested in working in the government sector, your GS rating will help you to determine your starting salary. Government positions offer pay scales based on education, security ratings, and other factors.

A salary discussion will generally take place during the stage of inquiry. Sometimes employers may ask you to list salary requirements in the cover letter or application. The employer wants to know if they can afford you. If they can't, they won't bother interviewing you any further. Do your homework; the payoff can mean the difference between working one job or two! Know what you need before you begin. Let me suggest you tap into websites such as: www.payscale. com or www.salary.com to give you a head start.

Just like your interview preparation and anticipation is what is required. Keep in mind that salary discussions today come in a number of different formats. They may begin before the interview, during the interview, and sometimes after, when they are more likely to extend an offer. You are not always required to give a definite figure; stick with a salary range instead.

Discussions should never include your kids, your plastic surgery, or your divorce. It needs to be centered on your abilities and your value. There's no format in how and when the negotiation will present itself; just be prepared when it does.

Sample Negotiation:

You've gotten the job offer and you are in the negotiation phase—yeah!! Before walking through the door, make sure you get a good nights sleep. What? Yes, that's important. If you ever negotiate when you're tired, angry, hungry, frustrated or desperate, ultimately you are at a disadvantage because your emotions are driving you and not your head.

Interviewer – Mark : "Angela, we are so excited about having you as a part of our team. The only remaining issue seems to be salary. Now, we are working with a limited budget, but we can offer you $___ as a starting salary. After your six-month review, we can look at increasing your salary another 15 percent within your first year if we have the money."

If the figure is in the ballpark, let the employer know that you are ready to get started; just pick the date. If the figure seems low, you can try saying something like this:

Angela: 'That sounds great. But I'll be honest with you, Mark. I think the responsibilities for this position are pretty extensive considering I'll be managing three sites as well as 40 staff. I've given this some thought. I would need to start between _____ and _____ within that salary range. Of course, I am flexible if other compensations are being offered.

Or you can say . . .

Angela: Mark, I did some research for this position and the average starting salary is between $_____ and _____. If we can get within this range, I think that is something I can work with.

Obviously, you need to put this in your own words, but the general idea is to get the employer to give you the information first so that you can do a little research and respond. Now, the employer may disagree and refuse to raise the salary to the amount that you were hoping for. But that doesn't mean you can't come up with a counter-offer. Only you know what it takes to meet your financial needs for yourself and your family. Just keep in mind that everything is negotiable.

> *Asking questions creates the atmosphere for a conversation.*

Know When to Accept the Offer

Regardless of the demand for your particular skills in the job market, no one wants to hire an applicant whose sole interest appears to be money. The key to balancing your needs and the organization's needs is to establish a cohesive relationship. Not every employer will be able to accommodate your needs. Give yourself some time to 'digest' the offer mentally and emotionally before giving the okay. Dissatisfied employees eventually become unproductive employees.

Be Prepared for Objections!

If the offer doesn't meet your standards, try the following:

- Ask for a specific salary and negotiate a salary review after ninety days on the job.
- Add that you would like the opportunity to prove yourself.
- State the salary range you require for this position.
- Discuss your ability to accomplish specific job objectives.
- Express your strong desire to work with the organization.

Know your bottom line.

Knowing your bottom line is knowing what you can live with. If you know you need $39,000 a year in order to meet your financial obligations, accepting a position that only pays $32,000 is automatically going to bring you a year of stress. Begin your negotiations in the low- to mid-forty (assuming your skills, education, and experience are consistent with this range). Use concrete evidence to prove that you're worth the salary you expect.

Recognize your true value.

Consult reference materials online, trade publications, and other sources. *(use the websites listed on Part 14)* Researching the company in advance will definitely prove beneficial here. Demonstrate to the employer that you know where the company is positioned in the marketplace and that you have ideas about improving the company's position, products, and services. Use only your skills, experience, and vision for the position as justification for the salary you seek.

PROFESSIONAL ACTION PLAN

Now that you know, how will you grow?

I have designed this page to give you the opportunity to determine what valuable information you have received and how you can implement strategies discussed in this chapter.

1. _____

2. _____

3. _____

4. _____

5. _____

6. _____

PART 9

Building Opportunities For Promotions

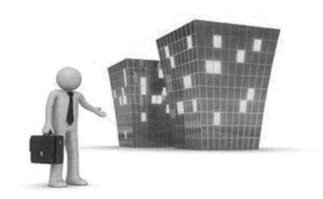

Getting Noticed For The Right Reasons!

CHAPTER 13

BUILDING YOUR PROFESSIONAL REPUTATION

You finally got the job. Everything it took to get the job paid off! What most people don't realize is that the first three to four months on the job will solidify future opportunities within the company. Every time your name is mentioned, it either builds you or destroys you. I continue to re-iterate that people don't tell you what they think of you; they tell others, right? Case in point:

Angela: "So, Steve, have you met the new guy?"

Steve: "Who, Martin? Yeah. I got a chance to meet him last week, and he seems to be pretty sharp. I think he's going to be a good fit with our division."

Marcel: "Are you talking about Martin?"

Angela: "Yes."

Marcel: "Yeah, I met Martin. He seems really nice. Did you know he used to work at yada, yada, yada division, and they said he really knew his stuff?"

And there it begins. When it comes to promotion, most people don't start at the top—unless they own the company. During your first three or four months, you develop a reputation within the company. As you grow to know and understand the industry, the culture, the people, and the process, your reputation will determine opportunities for growth within your company.

By laying the groundwork early on in your tenure with a company, you prove yourself an asset. Then others will see your potential, and that's where career building takes off. You will STAND OUT, get ahead, and get noticed.

Success is not just about how smart you are, how much you know, or even who you work for. The key word is *influence. Webster's New Riverside Dictionary* defines the words as "the power to produce effects, especially indirectly or through an intermediary. 2. The condition of being affected. 3. One exercising indirect power to sway or affect."

Of course, I'm not suggesting you go into a new job and scope out the director's office. I'm saying that during the first three or four months of your job, your employer will be looking at your potential. Typically, employees make the most effort when they're new in a position, in order to prove themselves. Think about it. When you meet someone at a fundraiser, you are looking for opportunities to network and connect with someone—and yes, the concept is the same, regardless of the industry. Whether it's personal or professional, it makes no difference.

Here are several examples:

A coach goes to scout out a basketball player. The player has an opportunity to make the team if he or she can STAND OUT.

You meet someone at a lunch meeting—there's an opportunity to do business with the company if you STAND OUT.

Even if you go to the pet store, there is always one pet that – you got it – STANDS OUT.

You understand my point. The one thing I hope you learn from this chapter is that people are constantly watching and evaluating your efforts. The point is you must excel in a way that gets noticed and STAND OUT!

Every conversation is an opportunity for you to grow and build relationships.

Is there a negative to influence? Well, there can be. Let's say you're working with someone who's been with the company over a period of time, and you begin to hear comments like 'I've been here for twelve years, and nobody has ever said…yada yada to me!' This can be measured in two ways. It may be that this employee has given up trying to leave a mark. Or this person has lost hope that success is possible.

Working hard is not what gets people promoted; people get promoted when they work to achieve something of value. There's a delicate balance involved in striving for promotion. Some of the very people who trained you when you first joined the company believe you owe them a debt of gratitude, and will sometimes use this as a reason to sabotage you. Build your reputation using the four keys we talked about in the beginning of the book. Remember? They are:

- ◆ professional communication skills
- ◆ willingness to learn
- ◆ ability to work with others
- ◆ solid work efforts and attendance

Strategies to help you STAND OUT:

Acknowledge people by name. "Good morning, James" can be one of the most powerful phrases in the English language. Nothing means more to people than being acknowledged. That's why nametags are so important. When you greet someone, it sends the message "You are important and you deserve my attention." It is not simply about common courtesy. Not recognizing people leaves a poor and lasting impression. (By the way, eye contact and head nods are also forms of acknowledgment.)

Become an expert. Have you ever heard the cliché "Jack-of-all trades, master of none"? I would rather be the master of one thing and delegate the rest to others as needed. Once you excel in one area, you set yourself up to be recognized as the best.

Celebrate others' successes. "Hey, Bonnie, nice job on that proposal! The staff thought it was great." I assure you that when you walk away from Bonnie, she will feel good every time she sees you. Why? Often, people only notice problems or errors. The fact that you let Bonnie know that she made something happen (and you took notice) means she will produce more. Kids are the same way. Let them know they did well with their grades, and they will do everything they can to make it happen again.

Take the lead on a project. Anytime you take the lead, it causes other to see you differently. I enjoy watching *The Celebrity Apprentice*. It just goes to show that being a celebrity doesn't automatically make a person a good leader. The key to a project's success falls on the shoulders of its leader. Of course, every project may not be a successful one. But don't negate the fact that others notice your tenacity to keep trying.

Do something for someone unexpectedly. Have you ever had someone ahead of you pay your toll? Because it was unexpected, it was a nice surprise during the day and chances are you told someone else about it too! It's the same concept of receiving an unexpected gift. The principle behind celebrating other people's successes is at work here. Offer a hand when it's not required. Ask others if there is anything you can do to help.

Acknowledge other people's families. Everyone works for something. I know, I know; everybody tells me it's just to pay the mortgage. Okay, you're right. But the other reason people work is to take care of their families. "Tammie, how was the graduation?" That kind of question means you may have to listen to Tammie talk about the ceremony for half an hour, but it builds rapport, because you thought enough to ask. It also allows you to find something you may have in common. Again, this is another way to STAND OUT.

Interact with coworkers after work. Hold on, hold on; I know what you are thinking: "I don't know these folks!" You may not be comfortable socializing with coworkers after work. However, whenever your company has structured social events, it's important to be there. You don't have to devote your time to someone you're not fond of or drink until you pass out, but it is important to attend company-sponsored social events. It has been my experience that when you don't attend, others may presume that you are egotistical. Simply showing up is another way for you to bond with coworkers.

Prepare for your first ninety-day evaluation. At some point, your work will be evaluated against a set of standards, and become a powerful tool to future opportunities. Anticipate that your employer will probably base your review on the your productivity, enthusiasm, and your ability to work cohesively with others. This is where your working relationships make the difference. I'm not recommending suckin' up, but it ain't gonna' hurt, right? I'm kidding of course. But look at it from this perspective: everybody can find room for improvement.

CHAPTER 14

MYSPACE, YOUR SPACE, OUR SPACE

Ahhh the joys of technology. We simply can't do without it. It supports us in every area of our lives; from getting directions to printing coupons for grocery shopping. Oh, yeah and finding a job. So, what does that have to do with *my* Facebook page? Everything!

Do you have a Facebook page, Twitter or LinkedIn account? I did a blog entitled: *What's done in the dorm will come to light.'* Hey, I get it, it's your final year in college and your graduation is right around the corner – let the celebration begin! Your friend just got a promotion – that's great. You're at a professional football game – cool. In any of these situations it's a social environment which may involve late night parties, tailgates, dorm keggers, drinks at the restaurant . . . . whoooaaa, not so fast my friend. While it may be a social occasion, always remember in our digital society, what you do can and will be used against you in the employment arena.

Does it mean that you can't have a beer or hang out with your friends? No, but what you do with your friends can work it's way into your professional file. Think about how many cyber-social media sites exist today. All of them somehow tap into one another and can easily be accessed by potential employers when you apply for a position. We all know that when you apply for a job a background check is eminent. That means *all* of your information must be given, not just your grades and employment history. Companies are now taking this a lot more seriously than ever before. Employers now have staff to research all of its potential candidates.

A powerful article was written in the N.Y. Times in June entitled: "The Web means the End of Forgetting" is a shock of how often this rule is being utilized and how damaging it can be to ones future. People are being terminated left and right because of information that is posted on their Facebook page. Just think of the number of politicians and other celebrities who have been ousted because of something posted online. Is it right? I guess that's based on your perspective. But this article posted in the New York Times is a huge indicator on where we are in our society as it pertains to the rights to 'free expression'.

Take a look:
http://www.nytimes.com/2010/07/25/magazine/25privacy-t2.html?ref=magazine

While the information highway has been an incredible asset to our society, it is also the most dangerous because it's done behind a keyboard. Identity theft, pedophilia, sex scams and more all at the click of a button and without putting a face to the crime. So, what does all this have to do with me? You need to remember your webpage, email, Twitter account and every other online resource is a walking tabloid complete with recorder and camera.

Our college years are probably where most of our experiences are created and then broadened. Everything from travel to relationships usually begin in our college years. What this means is to be cautious of who you hang out with, what you do in your personal conduct and how you are building your reputation. For me personally, the same concept was pervasive in my military career. As long as you served the military, there was an expectation that your personal life reflects your respect for the uniform.

Oh, by the way, I'm using the analogy of the college environment, but as we age, this same information is also being documented related to your credit report, banking information, driving record, bankruptcy, child support or anything else related to personal character. The internet is a snapshot of time. Your college years are as well. It is a portion of your life to get you to your working career. When employers research you online, they are also researching your history, your character, your experiences, and your *future*!

Keep this in mind the old saying of: 'if you wouldn't do it in front of your Mom, then don't do it at all.' Don't worry about Mom. In today's society it should be: 'if you wouldn't do it on American Idol, then don't do it!'

PROFESSIONAL ACTION PLAN
Now that you know, how will you grow?

I have designed this page to give you the opportunity to determine what valuable information you have received and how you can implement strategies discussed in this chapter.

1. _____

2. _____

3. _____

4. _____

5. _____

6. _____

PART 10

Employment Dilemmas

What Do You Do If...

CHAPTER 16

EMPLOYMENT DILEMMAS: WHAT DO YOU DO IF...

T his chapter gives you an opportunity to test your professional savvy in handling real-world work scenarios. Keep in mind that every scenario may not come up with the *exact* same answer every time. These dilemmas are just designed to make you think on your feet to handle potential issues.

Make this fun by playing the game with friends, family, coworkers, or even folks in your job club. Have fun!

EMPLOYMENT DILEMMA

The Scenario

You're on your way to the interview, and —oh no—there's been an accident. You know you're going to be late, though you have no idea how late. This interview is a once-in-a-lifetime shot. Do you…

a) Call and let your interviewer know you're running late.
b) Try to get to the interview as soon as possible.
c) Ask the interviewer if he or she would be willing to reschedule based on circumstances.

Most people respond that the best answer is to call and let the interviewer know about the accident. If they just think you're running late, employers have made it clear to me, they think that it's within your control to be on time.

Keep in mind the interviewer may have other appointments scheduled. The employer needs to decide what happens next. Calling in is a no-brainer, but after that, the decision is in the employer's hands.

What else could you do?

_____
_____
_____
_____
_____

(These scenarios are not real and are not meant to offer legal advice as it concerns the workplace. Always consult your HR director before taking any action.)

EMPLOYMENT DILEMMA

The Scenario

You see an advertisement for an office manager online. The advertised position lists "low $30s" as the salary, and you only have three years of experience in the field and no degree. You believe you deserve $6,000 more. How would you negotiate the salary?

a) Make a case that you're worth the increased salary.
b) Let the employer know that you could probably get the salary you want elsewhere.
c) Take the job and earn the extra increase.

Two of these answers could do the trick. First, do your homework and find out as much as possible before your interview. Understanding all of the factors can help in determining your answer. Most important, know your bottom line.

What else could you do?

_____

_____

_____

_____

_____

EMPLOYMENT DILEMMA

The Scenario

In the middle of your evaluation, your boss is called away. She left out your personnel file, and you notice a discrepancy. What do you do?

a) Say nothing. Your boss may get upset.
b) Ask to see your personnel file.
c) Tell your boss that you looked at your file and noticed a discrepancy.

Consider how you would feel if someone were looking on your desk without your knowledge. Wouldn't you wonder if this person had looked at other things? As you go through your review, you will legally be given an opportunity to review and sign it. At that time, you can bring up the discrepancy.

What else could you do?

_____

_____

_____

_____

_____

EMPLOYMENT DILEMMA

The Scenario

You are a sales representative for a distribution company. A coworker promised to deliver his or her merchandise within two weeks of your order, but it hasn't arrived. The customer is livid and is taking it out on you, but it wasn't your fault. Do you...

a) Make it clear to the customer that the error was not your fault.
b) Stay calm and promise to look into it personally.
c) Get angry with the customer—who do they think they're yelling at?
d) Promise a discount on the customer's next purchase.

Composure is critical to this situation. It's natural that you'd want to return fire on the customer, but we've been told the customer is always right. Saying you'll talk with the manager may not work either; the manager may not be available, and people want results immediately. The customer really doesn't care whose fault it is; he or she just need to hear the words *"Here's what I can do."*

What else could you do?

_____

_____

_____

_____

_____

EMPLOYMENT DILEMMA

The Scenario

How do you get Margaret, who is close to retirement, to do her work rather than talk about retirement all the time?

a) Suffer through it until she retires.
b) Put something in her coffee.
c) Work with her and gain her knowledge.

Let's be honest; you can't force people to work, especially when they are mentally on their way out. If retirement is a long way off, learn all you can from your coworker and then avoid her like the cold when she starts rambling.

What else could you do?

_____

_____

_____

_____

_____

EMPLOYMENT DILEMMA

The Scenario

Alicia, who has previously helped you find work is now in need of a job. You've heard that she's had problems at her last job. What can you do to help her while discouraging her from working at your company?

a) Tell her there are no positions (even though there may be).
b) Offer to help her with her résumé.
c) Promise to give her name to the HR person.

First, there is more than one way to help someone find a job. Since she has helped you, there might be a subliminal expectation for you to return the favor. Letting her know you'll give her résumé to HR can show your support—just don't promise any results.

What else could you do?

_____

_____

_____

_____

_____

EMPLOYMENT DILEMMA

The Scenario

You're working with a boss who is really attracted to you, but you are not to them. They begin to press you to go out with them. This could affect your ability to get promoted. What would you do?

a) Let them know you are not attracted to them
b) Go out with them as a part of the team
c) Tell them you are already dating someone (even if you're not)

Considering we spend so many hours a day interacting with our coworkers/ supervisors, it's only natural to build close relationships with some of them. However, lying about a relationship will only cause distrust. My suggestion is to let them know you have professional boundaries. (except if it's Brad Pitt)

What else could you do?

_____
_____
_____
_____
_____

EMPLOYMENT DILEMMA

The Scenario

You work with Carl and discover that he earns more money than you do even though he essentially does the same job. What would you do?

a) Discuss it with your coworkers.
b) It's not your job to determine how much money someone should make.
c) Ask human resources about why there is a disparity in salaries.

Salaries aren't always determined by how much work people do. Pay scales are determined by a number of various factors including experience, education, position title, expertise and company budget. If you don't want people to discuss your salary, don't discuss others.

What else could you do?

_____

_____

_____

_____

_____

EMPLOYMENT DILEMMA

The Scenario

A coworker takes extra time at lunch every day. What can you do to avoid feeling animosity toward this person? Do you...

a) Take the situation to your director.
b) Talk to the coworker directly.
c) Take a longer lunch yourself.

This can be a sticky situation. Consider first that if it doesn't impact your ability to do your job, let it go! Folks spend too much time watching others during the day anyway. If it does impact your work, however, it's time to have a heart-to-heart with your colleague. Going to the director is a form of tattling. Handle the issue like adults and have a private discussion. If that doesn't work, then you can tattle.

What else could you do?

_____

_____

_____

_____

_____

EMPLOYMENT DILEMMA

The Scenario

Where do candidates make the most mistakes in the application process?

a) Cover letter
b) Résumé design
c) Interview follow-up

The interview went great, but you've heard nothing! Because people often believe the employer will call them if they are still interested, the candidate will sometimes fall down on the job when it comes to the follow-up. Pick up the phone, send a telegram or just a simple e-mail can get you what you need – an answer.

What else could you do?

_____

_____

_____

_____

_____

EMPLOYMENT DILEMMA

The Scenario

During your interview, you can tell that the woman you would be working with is going to be a pain in the neck. Do you...

a) Take the position and learn all you can.
b) Don't take the position at all.
c) Take the position and apply for other jobs.

Your financial situation is the determining factor here. It doesn't matter where you work—you will always have to work with "that" woman (or someone very similar), so get used to it. Lastly, if your car is about to be repossessed, being picky may not be an option. It's ultimately your choice.

What else could you do?

_____

_____

_____

_____

_____

EMPLOYMENT DILEMMA

The Scenario

Your boss asks you to doctor up the invoice for his or her expenses. You could lose your job if someone found out, or you could be written up if you don't. What do you do?

a) Do it anyway (your job is on the line).
b) Discuss it with HR.
c) Let him or her know that you are uncomfortable and won't do it.

No matter what you decide, you have to be willing to take the hit for your convictions. The discussion should address the repercussions of losing your job or the other consequences of your actions. Keep in mind, every discussion doesn't have to begin with HR. Keep the focus on your actions, not your boss's.

What else could you do?

_____

_____

_____

_____

_____

EMPLOYMENT DILEMMA

The Scenario

A staff intern spends a little too much time texting and tweeting at work. He's also the supervisor's nephew. What do you do?

a) Delegate tasks to him anyway.
b) Take the situation to his uncle.
c) Nothing. He's only an intern, and the supervisor won't do anything anyway.

A staff intern still gets paid to work like everybody else. The fact that he's the supervisor's nephew should have no impact on you. Give him the work he's paid to do!

What else could you do?

_____

_____

_____

_____

_____

EMPLOYMENT DILEMMA

The Scenario

A staff member consistently makes mistakes on his reports, and the supervisor keeps coming to you to 'fix' his mistakes. What do you do?

a) Talk with your supervisor concerning your workload and the fact it's overwhelming to take on additional work.
b) Suck it up and do it. It's really no big deal.
c) Tell your coworker that you won't do his or her work anymore.

After you curse out your coworker, then...

Discussing this matter with your manager is your first line of defense on this one. Why? Your manager probably doesn't realize how it impacts your other tasks. Your manager may not care that it does, but letting him or her know may be the easiest way to lighten your load.

What else could you do?

_____

_____

_____

_____

_____

EMPLOYMENT DILEMMA

The Scenario

A coworker spends too much time on the phone with his or her kids. What do you do?

a) Complain.
b) Discuss it with the supervisor.
c) Nothing.
d) Talk with your coworker.

Okay, this is one of the few scenarios that you may not want to see. What we tend to do is complain. But consider that the supervisor doesn't want to hear about it even if it is true. Unless it's detrimental to your coworker's work performance—I mean, *really* detrimental—the supervisor won't care. Just like we don't like it when people talk too loud on their phones, there's absolutely nothing we can do about it.

What else could you do?

_____
_____
_____
_____
_____

EMPLOYMENT DILEMMA

The Scenario

How do you deal with a coworker who likes to share way too many details about his or her personal health issues?

a) Mention it to another coworker.
b) Change the subject.
c) Explain to your coworker that the discussion makes you uncomfortable.
d) Run the other way!

People who share too much personal information are not aware that they're making other people uncomfortable. However, if you change the subject, it allows you to control the direction of the conversation. If your coworker insists on sharing personal details even after you have changed the subject, make it clear that the conversation needs to stop.

What else could you do?

_____

_____

_____

_____

_____

EMPLOYMENT DILEMMA

The Scenario

One of your clients is extremely arrogant and rude. This client brings in a substantial amount of money, but you have been told to let the account go. What do you do the next time the client is rude to you?

a) Use humor to make your point.
b) Nothing. Maybe your client is under a lot of pressure.
c) Address the issue and let the client know that rude behavior is not acceptable.

You can address anything with the right amount of diplomacy. Standing up for yourself doesn't have to mean combat. However, a professional attitude in addressing rude behavior is about self-respect. Of course, hiring a hit man maybe another option with a payment plan.

What else could you do?

_____

_____

_____

_____

_____

EMPLOYMENT DILEMMA

The Scenario

A well-respected colleague has invited you to a client's annual Christmas party. You've been working late, you're exhausted, and you still have a report due for a college course the next day. What do you do?

a) Show up anyway. You can stop in to connect with your colleagues for a moment.

b) Contact them and explain you won't be able to attend.

c) Don't worry about it. It's not your party, so people won't notice you weren't there.

Showing up doesn't mean moving in. Understand, though, that accepting a drink usually means staying later than you initially planned. Give yourself a time frame (say an hour), spend some quality time with your colleagues and client, and then bow out gracefully, but prepare yourself for an all-nighter!

What else could you do?

_____

_____

_____

_____

_____

EMPLOYMENT DILEMMA

The Scenario

Your colleague has been ill for several weeks and her work has shifted to your desk. It's really too much for you to handle. What do you do?

a) Stay later so you can catch up.

b) Drop hints that you are overworked.

c) Use this as an opportunity to show your stuff.

d) Ask for additional support.

Let's be honest: how many of you would just stay later to catch up? That's our natural instinct, because we don't like to admit we need help. But if you know it's been several weeks and could be several more, don't try to be a superhero at the expense of your health and family. Do your best, but ask for support. There's no reason that you can't do both. Asking for support doesn't mean incompetence; it's called wisdom.

What else could you do?

_____

_____

_____

_____

_____

EMPLOYMENT DILEMMA

The Scenario

You've been planning to go on vacation for the past six months, but one of your supervisors suddenly insists that you can't because you need to work on an important project. What do you do?

a) Reschedule your vacation after the project's due date.
b) Come in early, stay later, and work to complete the project before your trip.
c) Take your scheduled vacation.

This is a pretty simple dilemma, as far as I'm concerned. First, if you've been planning a vacation for six months, you probably won't be able to get a refund on the airline tickets, hotel expenses, etc. Not to mention that you wouldn't be the only one affected by this situation—there's also your family to consider. Is it fair to them to reschedule? Second option: do what you can for the project, and prepare to have a backup during your absence.

What else could you do?

_____

_____

_____

_____

_____

Every resolution begins with a solution.
It's the professional you that everyone is watching!

PROFESSIONAL ACTION PLAN

Now that you know, how will you grow?

I have designed this page to give you the opportunity to determine what valuable information you have received and how you can implement strategies discussed in each chapter.

1. _____

2. _____

3. _____

4. _____

5. _____

6. _____

PART 11

EMPLOYMENT BARRIERS:

Transitioning after Incarceration, Addiction,

Mental Health Issues or Other Challenges

CHAPTER 21

BATTLING UNWANTED STIGMA AND STEREOTYPES

In this chapter, we will target job seekers who suffer from negative stigmas and stereotypes; particularly those transitioning from incarceration, addiction, mental illness or other barriers. Interviews in and of themselves are tough enough, but let's be honest, when you add in stigma it brings a whole new set of dynamics into the process. By offering you strategies up front, it will help take the sting out of the interview process by understanding your audience and taking you from obstacle to overcomer, from addict to advocate and from mental illness to mental wholeness. The definition of the word *'stigma'* is the shame or disgrace attached to something regarded as socially unacceptable.' Stigma is mental, but it shows itself in the physical. Before I began doing seminars and writing about the challenges of finding employment, I worked with a population of people whose stigma of mental illness brought a sense of fear going to the workplace. Stigma perpetuates itself as a label when those who don't understand it believe the stigma first rather than getting to know people as individuals.

The stigma must stop within our own thinking before it will stop in others. I believe one of the most effective ways to avoid it is to focus on your value and not your label. I can hear someone out there right now saying, 'I tried it, and it doesn't work. People still won't give me a chance'. No one needs to give you a job, you negotiate for it. Next and even more importantly, you have to begin with a 'rebuilding' concept. That's redesigning a new vision and a new direction for employment.

Later in the chapter I have a list of phrases to help support you in your bid for the 'yes'. I recommend that you master these phrases so the next time you are interviewing, you can utilize them until you develop your own.

We all know that knowledge is power, right? But knowledge is only power if you *apply* what you know! (I just made that up. I thought that was pretty good.)

Every 'no' gets you closer to the 'yes' you've been waiting for!

Hiring From the Employers Point of View

Okay, you're one of nine applicants for a job in the government and need to hire three new employees. One has a degree in economics, lives in the local area and has eight years of experience in the field. The second candidate has 18 years' experience, has worked in positions as executive director and was previously the manager for a division. The third candidate has an arrest record and served five years in prison. So . . . who would be the most likely candidate for an interview or even the job? I think it's a no-brainer.

One of the main issues is the natural negative frame of mind of our society. Where does that mindset stem from? From television shows to the news, programs like *'Law & Order', 'Criminal Minds, Without A Trace, Breaking Bad'* and the list goes on and on. These programs almost seal the deal in terms of a willingness to see anything other than fear in allowing people with a criminal history into the workplace.

"A survey of employers in five large cities found that 65% would not knowingly hire an ex-convict. Many would not be allowed to do so legally anyway. Another facet of the "tough on crime" movement has been to exclude ex-convicts from certain kinds of employment. In Illinois, ex-felons are banned from some 57 different professions, including such jobs as manicurist and barber, says

Diane Williams, president of Chicago's Safer Foundation, a non-profit organization that helps ex-offenders."

Often people are most comfortable about that which they know and understand. Remember the stigma itself is what drives the relationship. Because they don't understand how or why someone would commit a crime, it immediately brings up an unusually high level of fear and distrust. Employers need to understand that there is a benefit to hiring someone who is an ex-offender.

The U.S. Department Labor (DOL) and related agencies offer two major types of incentives for employers: bonding programs and tax incentives. "Incentives for hiring ex-offenders DOL's Federal Bonding Program provides fidelity bonds to employers hiring at-risk individuals at no cost to the employer. The bonds guarantee honesty for "at-risk," hard-to-place job seekers and cover the first six months of employment. One of the first websites I would visit along with those already recommended on the Appendix page is www.iseek.org/exoffenders.

The Benefits of Tax Credits

Often what those seeking employment aren't aware of is that tax credit benefits offer opportunities to individuals with disabilities, mental illness, or other possible barriers and disadvantages. One organization to look into is the DAV – the Disabled American Veterans or www.DAV.org which offers credit available to businesses who hire qualified vets before December 31, 2013. The $9,600 credit is part of the Work Opportunity Tax Credit (WOTC) and is included with other business related credits on the Form 3800, *General Business Credits*. Yes, you as an employer may get a tax credit up to almost $10,000 for hiring some of the most qualified experienced workers in the market today."

Special Populations with Added Challenges

I entitled this segment as 'special populations' because it focuses on job seekers who require additional support within the local community and within the government. In most cases the person is up against issues related to physical or learning disabilities, mental health challenges, language barriers, unemployed, underemployed, welfare recipients or even disabled veterans. Those in need of financial support receive (SSI) Supplemental Security Insurance or (SSDI) Supplemental Security Disability Income. Both SSI and SSDI are federally funded programs which provides financial support for housing, transportation and other essential needs.

In essence, your "disadvantage" may be an advantage because of the level of special support. Aside from the traditional methods we have addressed, the list below are organizations and government connections to investigate in applying. www.ssa.gov or

♦ Department of Rehabilitation Services
♦ Department of Health and Human Services
♦ Department of Veterans Administration
♦ Set-aside Government Jobs
♦ Welfare-to-Work Programs
♦ Vocational Rehabilitation Centers

So, let's go back to the scenario above about applying for the job in the government. Rather than simply send the paperwork and hope someone might look past the answer, take the proactive approach. Once you have the address in which to submit the application, go down to the office and hand-deliver it. When that is not an option, attach a letter to go with the application itself so that it offers more than just the simple résumé. The company may say, if you go to our website, you can apply online. You can apply *more* than once if you believe this is a great opportunity. Think about it this way: *'knock and the door shall be open. Seek and ye shall find'*. If it's listed not to contact other than online, then honor that.

When it is possible, just go into the office for the job, go to speak with someone. I'd like to call it a mini-interview. Ask them questions: How long have you been working here? Do you have a degree, yada, yada, yada. Again, there are additional questions listed on page 19.

Okay, here we are, you've answered all of the other questions with ease, until . . . . uh-oh, here it is. The question that always causes your stomach to turn.

Have you ever been arrested or served time in a jail facility?   If so, explain!

To say that the thought of leaving it empty wouldn't cross your mind is unrealistic. But as we all know, it's as simple as typing in your name and social security number and the truth comes out. So, rather than to give full details, you might try this approach.

Your answer would be: Yes.
Please explain: Would be happy to address this information privately within the interview.

It's really that simple. Can you do that? Yes, you can. First, it allows you to address the question honestly, and two, not expounding on details prevents the negative stereotype perpetrated by the stigma. On the next few pages, I have listed a number of power phrases to utilize in addressing this most uncomfortable question. But between the time you send the application and you get the call for the interview, brush-up on your responses and how to professionally prepare for the discussion.

Overcoming the Stigma of Incarceration
Everybody Deserves a Second Chance

Let me ask you something...have you ever gotten a speeding ticket? Ohhh com'on! Everybody has gotten at least one. I've gotten four but that's besides the point. I knew the speed limit said 65 mph, but my focus wasn't on my speed, I was distracted, lost focus, and wasn't paying attention. It's a blemish on my driving record, but once I paid the ticket, my life pretty much went on without much problem. But I was wiser the next time I got behind the wheel. My point is this; my driver's license shows that I have tickets, but it doesn't preclude me from driving. Everyone needs a second chance to pay for their wrongs and move forward with future opportunities.

Ex-offenders didn't plan their life's goal to be a criminal. But now that they've paid their 'ticket', it's time to rebuild their lives for a greater purpose. My hope is that anyone who reads this chapter will first look past their own stigma before others do. So, let's examine some of the areas you may be struggling with in the dilemma of finding employment beginning first with your self-esteem. Building your self-esteem is not easy, but it's crucial. If the inner you is locked into the stigma, the outer you will be too.

According to merriam-webster's dictionary ' *self-esteem* is *based on self-respect. A sense of personal worth and ability that is fundamental to an individual's identity'.* I like to say it this way: it's what the inner you and saying about the outer you.

As I previously mentioned joining networking clubs build your self-esteem because you are meeting new people on new terms. If you want to be better at who you are, position yourself around people who are better than you are, smarter than you are, more motivated than you are and willing to coach you or mentor you, says T.D. Jakes, a pastor of The Potter's House. 'Don't become incarcerated by your past! Change your perception and you'll change your opportunities.'

Next I have a list that identifies the obstacle and why people aren't hired with a difficult past. Your task is to evaluate which one of these challenges you may be struggling with and determine a strategy in address it.

Identify your obstacles before the interview, then strategize an alternative

- Addiction_____ Utilize AA and NA programs and find a sponsor_____

- Depression_____

- Fear of disclosure_____

- Housing issues_____

- Lack of computer skills_____

- Not enough money_____

- Lack of moral support_____

- Limited finances_____

- Transportation issues_____

- Negative Stigma _____

- Not enough education_____

- Low self-esteem_____

- Lack of communication skills_____

- Overwhelmed_____

♦ Volume of people competing for jobs_____

_____

♦ Résumés shows lack of experience_____

_____

Fear of not getting a job is no excuse for not trying

CHAPTER 22

THE ANSWER BEHIND THE INTERVIEW QUESTION

In the segment on the 'Imprint of Words', you will take note that there are certain words I recommended not to use because of the powerful imprint. In this segment there are also phrases that elicit a more positive response. For example, 'I'm sorry, I can't do that', implies that you will not make the effort. However, if you begin with the phrase .... 'unfortunately, I'm not able to do so', it implies 'I would, if I were in a position to do so.' You may not relate to those phrases in that manner, but make no mistake, people in the position of hiring do! The phrases I prescribe below acknowledges to the employer the positive as well as negative understanding of the position of the person. Again, just like the previous page, look at these phrases and determine which phrases seem to fit your ability to utilize them in a genuine way. The first set of the list acknowledges the situation, the second shows how to overcome it.

ACKNOWLEDGEMENT:

- I'm sure you have concerns and I would too . . . .
- Not excusing my behavior . . . .
- I was unwilling to listen. . . . .
- My negative attitude. . . . .
- I'm not proud of the fact . . . .
- Not blaming anyone. . . .
- If you will allow me. . . . .

- I'm not going to lie to you . . . .
- It's true that I struggled with drug addiction . . .
- I made the choice . . . .
- I didn't recognize . . . .
- Dropped out of school . . .
- Couldn't appreciate . . . .
- Poor decisions . . . .
- I was incarcerated . . . .
- Physical and mental challenges . . . .
- Didn't want to admit my problem . . . .
- Let me be honest with you . . . .

OPPORTUNITIES:

- Rebuilding my life and my career. . . .
- Demonstrate my skills. . . .
- Willing to prove myself . . . . .
- Moving forward . . . .
- I'm committed to. . . . .
- An important first step. . . .
- The new vision I have for my life. . . .
- Leave a positive mark . . .
- Gain your trust. . . . .
- New mindset. . . . .
- A second chance. . . .
- Fresh perspective. . . .
- Willing to invest . . . . .
- Renewed sense of hope . . . . .
- Understanding my background. . . . .
- Responsibility for my decisions. . . . .
- Clear direction . . . . .
- I recognize now. . . . .

- ◆ Hope to benefit. . . . .
- ◆ Believe in myself. . . . .
- ◆ Have a better appreciation . . . .
- ◆ I've done a self-evaluation . . . .
- ◆ Set realistic goals . . . .
- ◆ Waste this opportunity. . . .
- ◆ Constant improvements. . .
- ◆ Make this the turning point in my life. . . . .

Overcoming the Stigma of Disabilities and Other Barriers
Americans with Disabilities Acts (ADA)

The Americans with Disabilities Act of 1990 (ADA) is a law that was enacted by the U.S. Congress in 1990. It was signed into law on July 26, 1990, by President George H. W. Bush, and later amended with changes effective January 1, 2009.

Disability is defined by the ADA as "...a physical or mental impairment that substantially limits a major life activity." The determination of whether any particular condition is considered a disability is made on a case-by-case basis. Certain specific conditions are excluded as disabilities, such as current substance abuse and visual impairment that is correctable by prescription lenses. It was established to protect the rights of individuals with a physical or mental impairment that substantially limits one or more life activities such as eating, walking, seeing, hearing, breathing, working or caring for oneself.

The ADA is a wide-ranging civil rights law that prohibits, under certain circumstances, discrimination based on disability. It affords similar protections against discrimination to Americans with disabilities as the Civil Rights Act of 1964, which made discrimination based on race, religion, sex, national origin, and other characteristics illegal.

Okay, that's the official definition, but let's look at it from the employer's standpoint. Often people with disabilities are still seen as a 'handicap' that ultimately will cost them either money or productivity. Working in a diverse work environment is the new normal in the workplace. The Americans with Disabilities Act (ADA) covers a population of the workforce which can sometimes be overlooked for what can be perceived as the inability of an individual to work in a variety of working environments may be seen discrimination.

Non-Competitive Appointing Authorities: Individuals with a disability

Federal Employment Program with Disabilities - Individuals with disabilities (including severe physical disabilities, developmental disabilities and psychiatric disabilities) are eligible for excepted service positions within the federal government and are eligible to apply non-competitively to the agencies' merit promotion announcements.

In order to be considered eligible to apply to a merit promotion announcement based on a disability "Schedule A" you must have been certified by counselors of State Vocational Rehabilitation Agencies or the Department of Veterans Affairs. If you are applying based upon disability "Schedule A" eligibility at the State Vocational Rehabilitation Agency, or the Department of Veterans Affairs must certify your eligibility based on your ability to perform the essential duties of the job.

I'll be honest to say I am not an expert as it pertains to the entire process. However, if you visit www.ABILITYjobs.com, they have experts there who can walk you through the process step-by-step.

Overcoming the Stigma of Mental Illness
The National Alliance for the Mentally Ill (NAMI)

Unless you know or understand the term 'mental illness', it has a frightening misconception. The examples we have seen over the years include classic movies like *'The Shining'* or *'One Flew Over the Cuckoos Nest'* with Jack Nicoholson. And often times when heinous crimes are committed, the news media tends to drive home the point that the person may have had a mental illness.

Unfortunately, much like people with physical disabilities, people with mental illness often get placed in jobs we call the 3F's – food, flowers or filth which doesn't offer much in the way of opportunities to be paid living wages. Mental illness is not a debilitating life sentence. These issues can range from bipolar disorder, ADHD, schizophrenia, manic depression, panic attacks, post-partum depression or obsessive-compulsive disorder. 'Sixty-percent of people with mental illness want to work and two-thirds can do so successfully. Another 2% can hold down a job if they're given appropriate support says Mary Giliberti, Executive Director of NAMI, the 'National Alliance on Mental Illness.' Supported employment is another avenue employees with MI utilize in working together with 'peers'. Peers are others who have successfully gone through the transition of managing the emotional and overwhelming task of rebuilding their career with support.

Substance abuse can also mask itself within a dual diagnosis in that people are addicted to drugs and have a mental illness (even those who are homeless). If someone suffers from bipolar disorder they may become addicted to drugs in order to control or manage it. There are a number of organizations that specialize in support and advocacy for those with these challenges. Substance Abuse and Mental Health Services Administration or SAMHSA is another powerful advocacy group which seeks to advocate for better job opportunities, health care and/or housing for individuals recovering or struggling with mental illness.

My introduction to supporting individuals with mental health began in 1995 when I served as an employment specialist for a peer-run program named the Laurie Mitchell Empowerment and Career Center formerly known as (LMEC). Laurie Mitchell was a 31-year old mental health consumer who lived in the Northern Virginia area who was never able to realize her dream of finding employment because of the obstacles and the stigma. However, because of the program, the impact of her life will allow others to fulfill their dreams.

In 2007 LMEC was awarded the Secretary of Labor Freedom Initiative Award.

As you can see, I'm extremely proud to say that I served as the Board President from 2010-2014 and have seen it successfully flourish.

There are many celebrities who have experienced these issues first-hand and have built incredible careers including, David Letterman, Richard Dreyfuss, Catherine Zeta-Jones, Jim Carrey and Jon Hamm. I use celebrities in that they have *proven* that having an illness doesn't limit your abilities.

So, what would be an effective strategy to finding employment with MI? Serve on an advisory board, condo association, or even a homeless shelter so that people will develop a working relationship with you. Volunteer your time or work in a paid internship capacity with churches, or other with organizations who support those with challenges: English is a second language or hearing impairment. Remember, it's about building relationships with people who have like passions.

Keep in mind that as you develop these relationships, the people you work with are not your therapist, so disclosing your medical history is not the smartest thing to do. No, I'm not talking about hiding it, I'm talking about disclosure. I can hear you now. 'What's the difference?' *Disclosure* is choosing to address it privately with the people who need to know under your terms. *Hiding* is keeping the information to yourself with the hope that nobody finds out. Does that make sense?

But I haven't worked for an extensive period of time.

Okay, then you simply ask for accommodations. An 'accommodation' is considered any modification or adjustment to a job or work environment that enables a qualified person with a disability to apply for or perform a job. It could be as simple as adjusting your work hours or managing the stress levels of your work environment. I'm probably over-simplifying it, but there are a number of accommodations that exist. Don't be afraid to ask for what you're going to need to be effective. Determine whether this position will require any accommodations. This website on Mental Health America will offer you insight in terms of how to request these accommodations based on federal and legal requirements in your state. www.mentalhealthamerica.net

PROFESSIONAL ACTION PLAN

NOW THAT YOU KNOW, HOW WILL YOU GROW?

I have designed this page to give you the opportunity to determine what valuable information you have received and how you can implement strategies discussed in each chapter.

1. _____

2. _____

3. _____

4. _____

5. _____

6. _____

PART 12

Employment Barriers of Discrimination

CHAPTER 20

HOW TO ADDRESS DISCRIMINATION IN THE INTERVIEW

Have you ever watched the show *Jeopardy?* The premise of the show is to give the contestants answers and they must answer with the question. The contestants always seem to have the right answer no matter how difficult the question. Ahhh, but what I *didn't know* is that the contestants go through a strict regimen of study and literally living and breathing facts and information *before* they reach the stage of contestant. Recognizing and understanding discrimination will allow you first to identify it, and then to tackle these questions with finesse.

Discrimination under Title VII of the Civil Rights Act of 1964 (Title VII), prohibits employment discrimination based on race, color, religion, sex, or national origin. EEOC also encompasses job discrimination against lesbian, gay, bisexual and transgender individuals classified as a form of sex discrimination and thus violated Title VII of the Civil Rights Act of 1964

In the past ten years, discrimination has now begun to be recognized in a number of areas as it relates to individuals because of birthplace, ancestry, culture, or linguistic characteristics common to a specific ethnic group and not just people with disabilities.

On January 16, 2003 the State Legislature signed into law by the Governor in late 2002 the Sexual Orientation Non-Discrimination Act, typically known by its acronym "SONDA," which prohibits discrimination on the basis of actual or perceived sexual orientation in employment, housing, public accommodations, education, credit, and the exercise of civil rights. http://www.ag.ny.gov/civil-rights/sonda-brochure

As more and more laws are being passed, it is essential to understand how the state of which you live affects what rights you have in addressing these issues. That's why anything related to your Civil Rights in the workplace should be taken first to your HR, and then to seek legal remedies if you believe your rights have been violated.

These strategies will make the interview process easier for you to prepare so that people won't discriminate from hiring you. While, I'm not an EEOC attorney it can happen, and you should be aware of what to do, who to go to, and start living and breathing facts about the EEOC laws in your state, and prepare for the hard questions in advance.

Here we go!

If the interviewer says:
I noticed your application doesn't include any recent work experience.

HIDDEN QUESTION:
Why do you have so many gaps in your employment?

Potential answer could be:
In all honesty, I'm not proud of the fact that I was incarcerated. But I look at this opportunity as a chance to put my past behind me and start fresh.

Note: The biggest mistake job seekers make in answering this question is giving extensive details. This is not a court trial. The more detail you give, the more it sounds as if you are defending yourself.

If the interviewer asks:

Why were you incarcerated?

HIDDEN QUESTION:

Can you give me some details of why you did that sent you to prison?

Potential answer could be:

Actually, I was younger I was arrested for _____. But since my release, I've been working to pursue employment and focus more on rebuilding my skills. Has your company hired others who have been previously incarcerated?

Note: Don't spend too much time focusing on the details, but offer a simple explanation. When you ask the question it determines whether the company is amenable to hiring someone with a similar past experience.

If the interviewer asks:

Have you ever used drugs or been arrested for possession?

HIDDEN QUESTION:

What's the likelihood of you stealing or using drugs on the job?

Potential answer could be:

Yes, I was arrested for drug possession several years ago. I have successfully gone through drug rehabilitation. I've been working with a sponsor who has proven to be an incredible support throughout my rehabilitation.

If the interviewer asks:

It says you were fired from your last job. What happened?

HIDDEN QUESTION:

He or she wants to hear the full details of why you were fired.

<u>Potential answer could be:</u>

I was let go from my previous job because of a personality conflict with my direct supervisor. But I my secondary supervisor and I did work extremely well, and he was happy to write a letter of reference which I have given you.

Note: Never speak against a previous employer. It diminishes your professionalism.

<u>If the interviewer asks:</u>

Do you have any disabilities or require any accommodations for special needs?

HIDDEN QUESTION:

Are there any duties you will not be able to perform and how much will these accommodations cost ultimately cost them?

<u>Potential answer could be:</u>

I will need two accommodations. My previous employers provided _____ and it allowed me to complete my duties without any problem.

<u>Follow-up question (for you to ask the interviewer):</u>

My understanding is that this position offers accommodations. Is that correct?

Note: Don't present your needs as a negative issue, but an opportunity to enhance your performance.

<u>If the interviewer asks:</u>

It seems you have a number of gaps in your employment history.

HIDDEN QUESTION:

Why are you job-hopping?

<u>Potential answer could be:</u>

Unfortunately, the positions I've held were short-term positions. After funding was cut, and the position was eliminated. My goal is to acquire a position to build/rebuild my career and develop something permanent.

If the interviewer asks:

What would you say is your most important accomplishment? Your biggest failure or disappointment? Why?

HIDDEN QUESTION:

Do you know and understand yourself to admit your failures.

Potential answer could be: Okay, you're on your OWN for this one. Of course, I can't tell someone what to say because this is truly from a personal perspective. However, I might say something like this:

Note: I don't consider anything failures, but as teaching opportunities I don't want to repeat. ☺

When the interviewer asks:

Your driving record shows several DUIs . . . . .

HIDDEN QUESTION:

"What happens if we put you on our company insurance?"

Potential answer could be:

"Yes, I did receive several DUIs. So I specifically applied for this position because it does not require driving as part of the job." "Will that be the only criterion used in hiring for this position?"

When the interviewer asks:

Are you required to wear that based on your religion?

HIDDEN QUESTION:

"Do you have to dress like that all of the time?"

Potential answer could be:

"Yes. My faith is very important to me. However, at my last two jobs there have been no concerns as it relates to working with the staff or handling clients of diverse cultures."

Note: Keep the conversation on track to your abilities to handle the job and that previous employers have seen you as a professional.

Follow-up question (for you to ask the interviewer):

Are there any concerns that my beliefs might cause any issues?

What Do You Reveal in the Questions You Ask?

At the end of the interview or somewhere along the way, the employer will give you a chance to ask questions. *Always ask questions* and try to determine what kind of employee the interviewer is seeking and look for opportunities to sell yourself.

Let's do an assessment of a candidate who asked the questions below:

◆ May I ask what about my résumé drew your attention?
◆ What are the critical skills you're looking for to fill this position?
◆ Is this is a new position or will I be replacing someone?
◆ How do you see this position evolving over the next two years?
◆ What advancement opportunities exist for employees here?

Your impression of this candidate is:

_____

_____

_____

Come up with five other questions you might ask during an interview that would leave a positive impression:

_____

_____

_____

_____

_____

Employers are always impressed when applicants research the company before the interview and come prepared.

Let's do another assessment of a job candidate's questions here:

- ◆ My friend of mine said she makes...
- ◆ How many vacation days would I get?
- ◆ Do you allow smoking?
- ◆ Can I have a office with a window?

Your impression of this candidate is:

_____

_____

_____

_____

_____

_____

PART 13

Turning Conflict into A Working Relationship

With People You Don't Like

Working with Coworkers Who Make You Crazy

Consider that, at some point in your life, you will have to work with people who don't think, work, act, or perform the way you do. So what? From the moment you walked into the HR director's door, you said you could work with anybody. 'I'm a team player, 'you said, remember? The mark of a true professional is that you can work around your personal feelings to accomplish the job.

However, difficult people never believe they are difficult, because they consider their needs to be legitimate. They only see things from their points of view. People do what they do naturally. They don't intend to irritate people (even when they do), and they usually don't see the effects their actions have on others. You might compare them to two-year-olds, who don't try to be difficult. They don't wake up and think, "Hum, what can I do to stress them out today? I got it! I'll put something up my nose, so they'll have to take me to the hospital."

Let's get something straight: the people you work with are the same as the people you live with. We all have our issues. Case in point—we don't always put things back where they belong. We talk too much, or we talk too loudly on the phone. We forget to call people back. We don't always follow through on our promises. If you are disorganized before you get the job, you will be disorganized after you take the job. Our personalities don't turn to perfection once we get a job or a promotion.

When I served in the military, they emphasized the point that we needed to get along with everyone by making us change bunkmates every two weeks. The exercise trained us to work with others regardless of race, beliefs, personalities, intellect, or background. It worked! In combat, it doesn't matter whether you're left-handed or right-handed; it's about hitting the target.

You didn't like that person when you were in class together, so what if you get a position with him or her on campus? Is it likely that you'll change your mind about that person? Maybe not. Is it possible? Sure. But you won't find out until you work with them as an individual and not as a child. It's important to understand before you get into the working world that it's inevitable that you will work with people you don't like. However, liking everybody you work with is not a job requirement. Now, it is important that you come to understand the folks you work with, but it's not going to be easy. Remember, you're no picnic yourself!

Difficult People Never Believe They Are Difficult

To continue with our analogy comparing coworkers to little children, let's look at some more characteristics of children. Would you consider a child a difficult customer? Why not?

♦ Children are demanding.
♦ Children require extra attention.
♦ Children feel their needs are the only ones that count.
♦ Children won't let you alone until you meet their needs.
♦ Children cry out until someone takes action.
♦ Children constantly scream and complain about others (brothers/sisters).
♦ Children are the least likely to thank you after hours, days, and years of irritation.

Now, all you have to do is insert a person's name in place of "children," and yep, you've got it: that's your basic coworker.

Who would you consider a difficult client/customer/staff/director?

♦ Someone who is demanding.
♦ Someone who requires extra attention.
♦ Someone who feels his or her needs are the only ones that count.
♦ Someone who will not let you alone until you meet his or her needs.

♦ Someone who cries to someone (manager, director, shift supervisor).

♦ Someone who constantly screams and complains about everything.

♦ Someone who is the least likely to thank you after hours, days, and months of irritation.

Those are probably some of your future coworkers!

Moreover, remember that each of us brings into the work environment our own personality, generational thinking, gender, age, working style, and perceptions. We already have these characteristics before we walk in the door. Each phase creates difficulty for someone else. Let's see an example of this in action.

Difficult People are Based on Perspective

<u>Holly's side:</u> Richard really gets on my nerves. He keeps calling me into his office; it's like he doesn't know how to walk. He screams out the door as if he's lost his mind.

<u>Richard's side</u>: I never know when she's at her desk. She's either on the phone or gone somewhere.

<u>Holly's side</u>: If he would stop interrupting me, I could help the director finish this report. Then I'd be able to go home on time.

<u>Richard's side:</u> I just got out of a meeting with the director, and he expects this report by tomorrow morning.

So when Holly finally gets home, can you guess what she complains about all evening? Neither she nor Richard is aware that the director is the one driving them. They each believe the other is the difficult person. Richard this; Richard that. We don't always recognize that people aren't trying to be difficult, but the way they respond to pressure affects others.

I believe when it comes to handling difficult issues, whether inside or outside of the workplace, there are three basic options:

1. *Face it.* Acknowledge the issue.
2. *Fix it.* Come up with two options to deal with it.
3. *Forget it.* If you can't fix or change the issue, accept it.

And never let it happen again! But if it does, prepare yourself to find the answer that can help you cope with the situations in your work environment.

There are often situations that are simply out of our control. The more we try to control them, the more irritating, stressful, and overwhelming they become.

These suggestions might give you some concrete exercises to try. Every suggestion may not apply specifically to your scenario, but use the information when you need it. If it doesn't apply, let it fly. FYI: these are exercises you can do daily without hurting your back.

Don't Let Another Person Live Rent-Free in Your Head

I once worked with a woman named Angela (fictitious person), and people in the office could not stand her. Although she was the senior director of one of our divisions, people just did not respect her or her position. Unfortunately, she just didn't have the right people skills. She was smart and capable of doing her job, but she wasn't savvy when it came to interacting with people. She seemed to be sarcastic and to belittle people, and others assumed it was because she had a PhD.

From the moment she came into the office, people ignored her, talked about her, or treated her with phony politeness. To be honest, it was almost like high school. The interesting thing is that even when she wasn't in the office, guess what people did? That's right, they still talked about Angela. When Angela worked from home, people talked about her: "Who does she think she is?" When she missed staff meetings, people made bets about when she was coming back (if she came back at all).

The fact that people were still talking about her, even in her absence, said a lot about the impact she had on people. My husband once made a comment about her that gave me a true understanding of the phrase "letting someone live in your head." I was barely home and had just sat down for dinner when—I don't know how—the conversation turned toward Angela. I guess at some point, my husband got tired of hearing this woman's name, and he said, "Why don't we set a place for Angela, because you seem to bring her home every night for dinner!" What?

That was one of those "aha" moments. From that point on, I never mentioned Angela's name when I wasn't working. Not only did I remove her from my head; I removed her from my mouth.

> *Peace is not the absence of conflict, but the ability to cope with it.*

Don't Try to Change Other People

The key to being noticed and getting promoted is to work with people as they are. I believe the same principle applies to every area of life: marriage, children, friends, parents, and particularly the people we work with. But imagine if you work with someone who majored in chemistry and speaks in "chemistralian" (my new word). There will definitely be a major breakdown in communication. Rather than being angry that your coworker can't understand you, find a common ground where you can communicate so there is less likelihood of conflict. Focus on creating opportunities for cooperation.

Although we all know this to be true, it's hard to implement what we know when we are emotional. Here's an example from my own life that illustrates that point.

My husband and I are complete opposites when it comes to household maintenance. My military upbringing trained me so that I never left any clothes, shoes, toys, newspapers, magazines, mail, or trash on the floor. *(I leave the house what I'd like to call 'guest ready')* My husband, on the other hand, can walk by something with a stench and never notice the food moving on the floor. So the first few years of my marriage were full of battles: "Why can't you pick your stuff off the floor! Next time, I'll just throw it away."

It wasn't the loving abode I had dreamed of. More than that, yelling and complaining weren't getting me the results I wanted. So, in taking my own advice, I decided to hire someone who was happy to pick up after my husband and to keep our home up to my standards. Problem solved. The workplace environment calls for the same level of thinking. In some cases, there will be simple resolutions, and in others there may not be. The question is: Are you willing to quit your job to make a point to the other person? I thought so.

So—this applies equally to people you love and people you work with—let other people be themselves. Try not to remake others in *your* own image. Recognize that everyone doesn't have your same level of *anything* that you do. That's why it will always be an unfair comparison. If you stop trying to change people into you, they will have an easier time just being themselves!

Give Yourself Permission to Turn the Day Off

Set aside a time each day when you stop working. By setting a time to stop, it will put yourself on that schedule that you love to keep daily so you can feel like it's something you have accomplished. (Personally, I like 7:00 p.m.)

- ◆ Don't go upstairs in your home office and look over a few things.
- ◆ Don't check your e-mail or text anyone after that time – work related.
- ◆ Don't read over something.
- ◆ Don't just get "one more thing done." And last but not least
- ◆ Don't talk about Mike, like, or Ike after you leave the building.
- ◆ It's like taking the person home with you when you bring them up.

Give your family the best of you, not what' left of you!

Let It Go: There's Always Tomorrow

I used to say, "That's it. I'm gone." I'd leave everything at work only to realize that I may have left something at the office. Although it was 6:30 when I left (I was supposed to leave at 5:00), there I was trying to find a piece of paper for the next day. If I had recognized that the paper I was looking for would still be there the next day, I would have had a lot more time to spend with my family. There will always be something else you can do today. But if it were really that important to do, you would have done it already.

Don't Give Anyone the Power to Ruin Your Day

The guy in front of you was driving so slowly that you could have walked to your destination faster. The woman from accounting has asked you for the third time for paperwork that you've already given her. Then you find out your paycheck didn't get deposited. What else can go wrong!

As I said before, it doesn't matter what kind of day you are having; your attitude will determine whether it turns out to be a good day or a great day. Does it really matter that your coworker doesn't say good morning to you? Not really. I can promise you that you'll still be breathing at the end of the day whether it happens or not. Turning conflict into cooperation is the process of determining in advance how you choose to master the conflicts that occur in every area of your life, not just your professional life.

Well, there you have it. It is my hope and prayer that my book has given you insight and wisdom that you can utilize to move you from where you are now to finding your opportunities in the workforce or moving forward in your professional career. Use the knowledge you now have. Now that you know it, how will you grow to utilize these tools to master the Career Building process that shows you How To STAND OUT, Get Ahead and Get Noticed!

All the Best and much success!

The Employment Lady

Is there an organization that you feel could benefit from holding a workshop, conference or seminar at their company or organization? Well, don't just sit there, give me their name, phone number and email address so I can reach out to them to get started. Be the gift that you can give to others to change their future.

NAME:_____

TITLE: _____

ADDRESS:_____

EMAIL:_____

PHONE:_____

PART 14

ONLINE RESOURCES TO GET YOU STARTED

www.ABILITYjobs.com	Supports individuals primarily physical disabilities
www.About.com	Articles and blogs relate to employment challenges
www.theAEAP.com	Association of Executive Administrative Professionals
www.AHACareerCenter.org	American Hospital Association
www.ag.ny.gov/civil-rights/ sonda-brochure	Attorney General Eric Schneiderman
	Sexual Orientation Non-discrimination Act (SONDA)
www.aviationrecruiting.net	Job placement for individuals in the airline industry
www.bls.gov	Bureau of Labor Statistics
www.careerbuilder.com	Job-finding techniques
www.careerplanning.about.com	Career strategist, career testing & job search
www.careeronestop.org/businesscenter	Targets ex-offenders and others with disabilities
www.employmentproject.org	Local jobs based on zip code
www.employmentguide.com	Self-structured job search

www.esgr.mil	Employer Support of the Guard and Reserve
www.fabjobs.com	Step-by-step guide to getting a job in any career of interest
www.findtherightjob.com	Find a job you'll love
www.felons.view-local-jobs.com	Job opportunities for ex-offenders
www.genuinejobs.com	1400 work from home jobs
www.futureproofyourcareer.com	Personality traits that connect to various jobs
www.HealthCareerWeb.com	Healthcare facilities around the country
www.Hiltonworldwide.com	Working in the largest hospitality for hotels
www.hiringamerica.net	Military spouses
www.Hotelcareers.com	Hotels with a number of other occupations
www.IAAP-HQ.org	International Association of Administrative Professionals for Executive Administrators
www.indeed.com	Local job opportunities based on zip code
www.iseek.org/exoffenders	Job opportunities for ex-offenders
www.ITClassifieds.com	IT professional experts
www.jailtojob.com	Job-seeking strategies for those transitioning from incarceration
www.jobalot.com	Search for a variety of top jobs
www.jobsforconvictedfelons.net	From convicts to careerists
www.jobsflag.com	Part-time jobs
www.jobhuntersbible.com	*What Color Is Your Parachute* registry

www.Jobsforfelons.com	Free help for felons with career transition
www.JobsRadar.com	Variety of positions, from military to manual labor
www.Jobs4point0.com	Targeted at job seekers over 40
www.LMEC.org	Laurie Mitchell Empowerment and Career Center for those struggling with mental health issues
www.mentalhealthamerica.net	Mental Health Wellness in the workplace and life
www.military.com/veteran-jobs	Military and veteran opportunities
www.momcorps.com	Career development and placement firm
www.monster.com	Finding jobs on every occupational level
www.myskillsmyfuture.com	Worldwide one-stop career database
www.NAMI.org	National Alliance on Mental Illness
www.nichejobs.com	Unique job opportunities
www.OfficeTeam.com	Career and salary information for administrators
www.onetonline.org	National occupational database, worldwide
www.OPM.gov	Office of Personnel Management federal jobs
www.payscale.com	Determines salaries for positions at all levels
www.salary.com	Salary comparisons with tax-rate measurements
www.skillcow.com	Free career test with instant results
www.ssa.gov/ssi	Social Security Administration for financial aid

www.SmarterPays.com	Pay scale analysis of positions within a mile radius
www.Snagajob.com	Local jobs along with great articles
www.sologig.com	Contract consultant projects or self-employed
www.theeverythinggetajob.com	*The Everything Career Tests Book*
www.testq.com	Test on what motivates you in the workplace
www.ebenefits.va.gov/ebenefits/jobs	Veterans Employment Center
www.USAjobs.com	Specializes in federal government jobs
www.vetjobs.com	Supports transition for active or reserve veterans

SUGGESTED BOOKS:

A. Bronwyn Llewellyn and Robin Holt. *The Everything Career Tests Book: 10 Tests to Determine the Right Occupation for You.* Jan 19, 2007.   A.. *The Everything Get-a-Job Book.*, Jan 19, 2007.

Benjamin, Susan F., *Perfect Phrases for Dealing with Difficult People*, McGraw-Hill, New York, NY 2008.

Farr, Michael. *Next Day Job Interview: Prepare Tonight and Get the Job Tomorrow:Help in a Hurry.* Jist Publishing; (October 1, 2008.

Farr, Michael and Laurence Shatkin, (*Today's Hot Job Targets: Find Careers and Cities with Big Job Growth.* JIST's Help in a Hurry. July 2007.

Keirsey, David. Please Understand Me: Character & Temperament Types, 5th ed. Del Mar, CA; Gnosology Books, 1984, Kroeger, Otto..*Type Talk*, Delacorte Press: New York, 1988.

Krannich, Caryle Rae, and Krannich, Ronald L. Krannich. *101 Dynamite Answers to Interview Questions*, Manassas Park, VA, 1997

Maxwell, John C., and Parrott, Les. *25 Ways to Win with People: How to Make Other People Feel Like a Million Bucks.*, Nelson Business. Nashville, TN, 2005.

McKay, Dawn Rosenberg Adams Media Corporation 2004

Runion, Meryl. *PowerPhrases: The Perfect Words to Say It Right and Get the Results You Want.* Cascade, CO, Power Potentials Publishing, Revised 2005.

Nadler Burton, *The Everything Job Interview Book: All You Need to Make a Great First Impression and Land the Perfect Job,* Impact,2006.

Nadler Burton, Jay Nadler, Justin Nadler *The Everything College Major Test Book: 10 Tests to Help You Choose the Major That Is Right for You,* Impact, 2006.

Oldham, John M. Personality *Self-Portrait: Why You Think, Work, Love, and Act the Way You Do.* New York, NY,:Bantam, 1990.

Schuman, Nancy, *1,001 Phrases You Need to Get a Job, The 'Hire Me' Words that Set Your Cover letter, Apart,* 2004,

<u>Yoshie Sano</u>, <u>Leslie N. Richards</u>, <u>Jaerim Lee</u>, January 2011, *Invisible Barriers to Employment: Mental and Behavioral Health Problems, Rural Families Work.*

What!!! Audiences are STILL talking?

Elaine Skowronski
A Terrific Idea

I wanted to thank you for turning things around for me. Your suggestion to give my boss a thank you note was terrific! It intrigued him as to why I did it and it began a very meaningful conversation and really improved our working relationship. That simple suggestion made a huge difference in turning things around and making this a win-win situation for both of us.

Lisa Skolnik
Unstoppable Woman

The seminar was an amazing experience for me. You are phenomenal! Powerful presence, engaging technique and confident. You have given me something that I will never forget and I will pass down to my daughters. How to become an "Unstoppable Woman!"

Pepper Sealy
I Can Believe in Me

I attended my seminar conference this summer, and you were the instructor. During the class you gave the suggestion to be assertive and we did the role play about asking for a promotion, something I've been trying so hard to do, but didn't know to ask. The next day I spoke to one of my supervisors; a month later, I got my promotion. Thank you for motivating me to not only believe in myself but to find a way to make others believe in me too.

Fonda Snyder
I've Never Learned More

I think Marja is not only fearless, but also flawless! Her ability to captivate and teach at the same time is impeccable. I feel she taught me a lot about how to get what I want and be effective in my communication techniques. I have found a new level of assertiveness. Marja is a complete ROCK STAR in her field!

Marja Lee Freeman is an international trainer, motivational speaker, facilitator, author, and employment expert. Her firm, M.L. Freeman Consulting LLC, has done seminars and conferences at colleges, universities, government agencies, church ministries and community programs. Her new DVD was just released entitled *Time Management Tune-Up*. Her husband, Donald, has traveled with her and supported her in all of her business endeavors. They have one daughter, Dawna Lee and live in Burke, Virginia.

Professional Career Development Programs:

♦ How to STAND OUT, Get Ahead, and Get Noticed!

♦ Résumé Designs That Work!

♦ The Question Behind the Interview Question

♦ Tips and Strategies for Getting the Most Out of Your Day

♦ Building Office Relationships for Staff and Management Excellence

♦ Turning Conflict into Cooperation: Working with People You Don't Like!

♦ 10 Steps to Career Success after Incarceration, Addiction, or Mental Illness

The Employment Lady

info@theemploymentlady.com
www.theemploymentlady.com
(703) 244-5677

21237564R00131

Made in the USA
Middletown, DE
23 June 2015